Editor
Lorin E. Klistoff, M.A.

Managing Editor
Karen J. Goldfluss, M.S. Ed.

Illustrator
Teacher Created Resources

Cover Artist
Brenda DiAntonis

Creative Director
Karen J. Goldfluss, M.S. Ed.

Art Coordinator
Renée Christine Yates

Art Production Manager
Kevin Barnes

Imaging
Denise Thomas
Nathan Rivera

Publisher

Mary D. Smith, M.S. Ed.

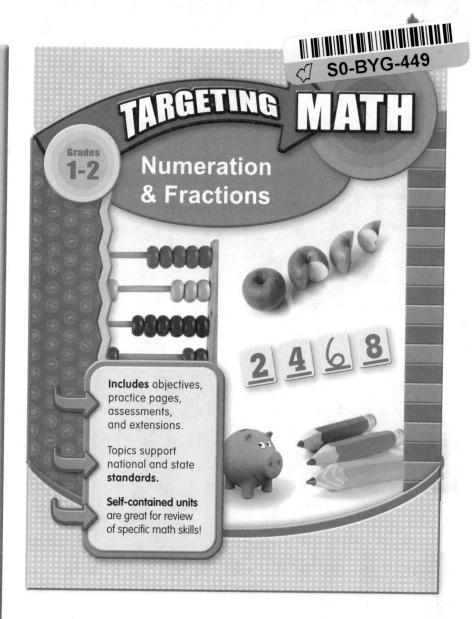

Authors

Nicole Bauer, June Fay, and Judy Tertini

(Revised and rewritten by Teacher Created Resources, Inc.)

Teacher Created Resources, Inc.
6421 Industry Way
Westminster, CA 92683
www.teachercreated.com
ISBN-13: 978-1-4206-8989-1

© 2007 Teacher Created Resources, Inc.
Made in U.S.A.

Table of Contents

Table of Contents

#8989 Targeting Math: Numeration and Fractions

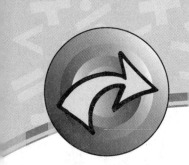

Introduction

Targeting Math

The series *Targeting Math* is a comprehensive classroom resource. It has been developed so that teachers can find activities and reproducible pages for all areas of the math curriculum.

About This Series

The twelve books in the series cover all aspects of the math curriculum in an easy to read format. Each level—grades 1 and 2, grades 3 and 4, and grades 5 and 6— has four books: Numeration and Fractions; Operations and Number Patterns; Geometry, Chance and Data; and Measurement. Each topic in a book is covered by one or more units that are progressive in level. The teacher is able to find resources for all students whatever their ability. This enables the teacher to differentiate for different ability groups. It also provides an easy way to find worksheets at different levels for remediation and extension.

About This Book

Targeting Math: Numeration and Fractions (Grades 1 and 2) contains the following topics: Numbers to 10; Numbers to 20; Numbers to 100; Numbers to 1,000; Calculators and Estimation; and Fractions. Each topic is covered by two complete units of work. (See Table of Contents for specific skills.)

About Each Unit

Each unit is complete in itself. It begins with a list of objectives, resources needed, mathematical language used, and a description of each student activity page. This is followed by suggested student activities to reinforce learning. The reproducible pages cover different aspects of the topic in a progressive nature and all answers are included. Every unit includes an assessment page. These assessment pages are important additional resources as teachers can use them to find out what their students know about a new topic. They can also be used for assessing specific outcomes when clear feedback is needed.

About Skills Index

A Skills Index is provided at the end of the book. It lists specific objectives for the student pages of each unit in the book.

#8989 Targeting Math: Numeration and Fractions

NUMERATION

These units work with numbers up to and including 20. Students are encouraged to demonstrate an understanding of the numbers through activities based on completing sets, matching groups to the correct numeral, and sequencing from zero to twenty. Drawing to complete sets, placing numbers in their correct positions, counting backwards, and following directions for ordinal numbers are all activities that further reinforce numeration skills. Skills include reading and writing the numbers in words and numerals. There are two assessment pages included.

#8989 Targeting Math: Numeration and Fractions

NUMBERS TO 10

Unit 1

Counting to 10
Sets
Sequencing

Objectives

- matches numerals to the appropriate group
- recognizes numerals 0 to 10
- makes groups of up to ten objects
- makes groups of a given size
- follows simple directions
- says numeral names in correct sequence
- recognizes numeral names zero to ten
- counts forward in 1s
- orders groups according to the number of objects they contain

Language

number, numeral, one, two, three, four, five, six, seven, eight, nine, ten, sets, groups, order, smallest, largest, match, correct amount, enough, before, after, between

Materials/Resources

sharp pencil, sharp right/left handed scissors, glue, paper clips, counters

Contents of Student Pages

* Materials needed for each reproducible student page

Page 8 Join the Numbers
matching toys to numerals; drawing lines from each numeral to its appropriate group of toys

Page 9 Picture the Number
looking at numerals and drawing enough pictures in each set to match the appropriate numeral

Page 10 Follow the Number Directions
looking at numerals and drawing enough flowers/spots/stars; circling the correct numeral

Page 11 Numeral Names
drawing objects to match the numeral name; writing correct numerals

Page 12 Counting on the Farm
looking at a picture, counting objects, and following directions

Page 13 Order the Sets
counting each set; correct sequencing from zero to ten (i.e., from smallest to largest); writing the correct numeral under each group

* scissors, glue

Page 14 Assessment

Pages 15 and 16 Bunny Hunt Activity
* pencils, paper clips, counters

Remember

❑ Before starting, each student needs to be able to refer to a resource in the classroom to form numerals correctly and to aid in counting (e.g., number charts).

#8989 Targeting Math: Numeration and Fractions

Additional Activities

- ❑ *Count Everything!—Count anything in sight such as pencils in the hand, windows in the room, books on a shelf, flowers in a vase, or small blocks on the table.*

- ❑ *Sing!—Sing action rhymes like "Ten in the Bed," "Five Little Ducks," "Six Sizzling Sausages," etc. Sing counting songs such as "This Old Man," "Ten Green Bottles," "Alice the Camel."*

- ❑ *Games—Play games such as dominoes. Make card games such as matching set to set, numeral to set, or numeral to numeral.*

- ❑ *Practice forming numerals correctly by tracing and copying.*

- ❑ *Make large number wall displays for students.*

Answers

Page 8 Join the Numbers

The following numbers should have a line to their connecting pictures:

> 3 = three cars
>
> 5 = five kites
>
> 2 = two trains
>
> 7 = seven pens
>
> 0 = circle with nothing inside
>
> 1 = one bear
>
> 9 = nine boats
>
> 6 = six airplanes
>
> 4 = four fish crackers
>
> 10 = ten basketballs
>
> 8 = eight hearts

Page 9 Picture the Number

The following should be drawn in each box:

> Row 1: 4 eggs, 7 circles, 10 stars, 6 squares
>
> Row 2: 1 star, 2 moons, 9 triangles, nothing
>
> Row 3: 8 plus signs, 3 hearts, 5 asterisks

Page 10 Follow the Number Directions

1. Eight flowers should be drawn next to the house on the left. Five flowers should be drawn next to the house on the right.
2. Nine spots should be drawn on the first dog, six spots on the dog in the middle, and four spots on the dog on the far right.
3. Two stars should be drawn in the box to the left, eight stars in the middle box, and one star in the box to the far right.
4. 9; 5; 4

Page 11 Numeral Names

The following pictures and numbers should be drawn:

> Row 1: three people drawn, 3; five people drawn, 5; no people drawn, 0
>
> Row 2: seven people drawn, 7; four people drawn, 4; eight people drawn, 8
>
> Row 3: two people drawn, 2; nine people drawn, 9; no people drawn, 0
>
> Row 4: six people drawn, 6; ten people drawn, 10

Page 12 Counting on the Farm

1. 9
2. 2
3. 4
4. 1
5. 3
6. 1
7. Make sure eight birds are drawn in the sky.

Page 13 Order the Sets

The order is as follows with the numerals written underneath:

> box with nothing (0), one elephant (1), two mice (2), three apes (3), four goats (4), five horses (5), six dogs (6), seven kittens (7), eight rabbits (8), nine fish (9), ten snails (10)

Page 14 Assessment

1. The following numbers should be matched to the following dominoes:
   5 to the domino with five dots, 6 to the domino with six dots, 7 to the domino with seven dots, 8 to the domino with eight dots, 9 to the domino with nine dots, 10 to the domino with ten dots
2. 7, 13, 10, 4
3.

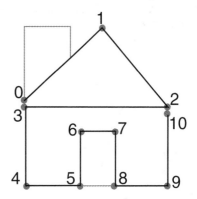

4. two = 2, one = 1, five = 5, seven = 7, ten = 10, six = 6, zero = 0, nine = 9, four = 4, eight = 8, three = 3

Name	**Date**

Join the number to its picture.

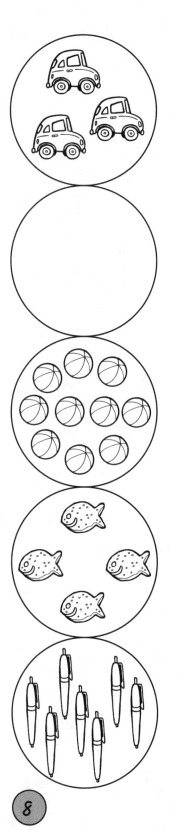

3
5
2
7
0
1
9
6
4
10
8

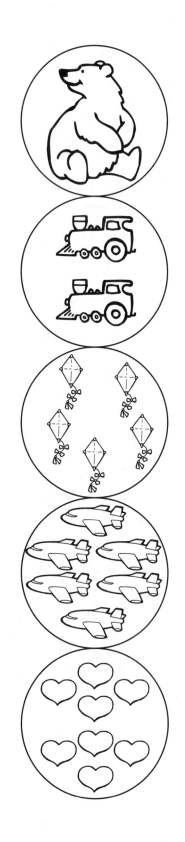

Name   **Date**

Draw the matching number of pictures in each box.

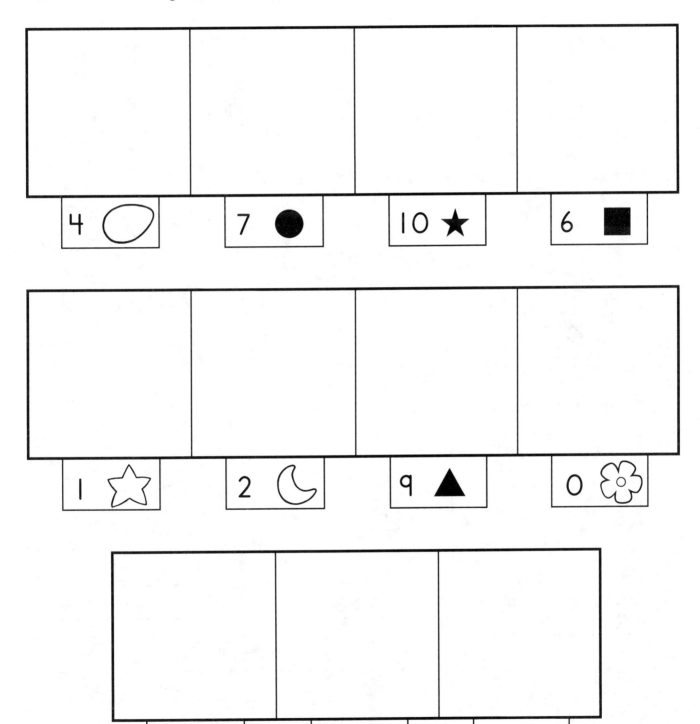

Name	**Date**

1. Draw the correct number of **flowers** in each garden.

2. Draw the correct number of **spots** on each dog.

3. Draw the correct number of **stars** in the sky.

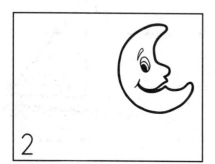　　

4. Circle the correct number for each group.

#8989 Targeting Math: Numeration and Fractions　　　　　　　© *Teacher Created Resources, Inc.*

Name

Date

Draw the correct number of people on each boat. Write the numeral on the sail.

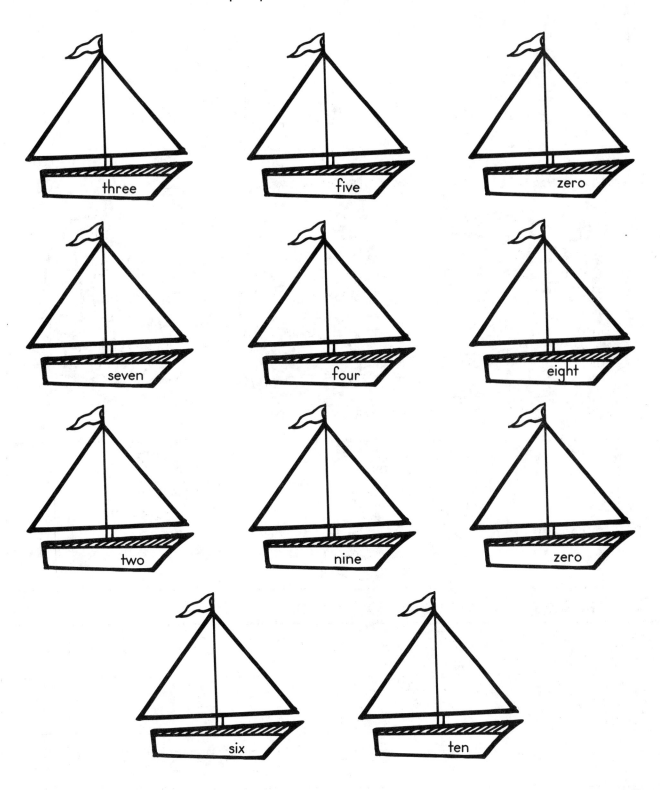

Name

Date

1. How many sheep? [   ]

2. How many cows? [   ]

3. How many people? [   ]

4. How many dogs? [   ]

5. How many horses? [   ]

6. How many bulls? [   ]

7. Draw 8 birds flying the sky.

#8989 Targeting Math: Numeration and Fractions

Name   **Date**

Cut out each set. Glue them in order from smallest to largest. Write the numeral under each set.

#8989 Targeting Math: Numeration and Fractions

Name	**Date**

1. Draw lines to match.

 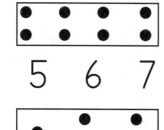 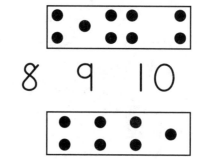 

5　6　7　8　9　10

2. Write the missing numerals.

6 ___ 8	12 ___	7 8 9 ___	___ 5 6

3. Join the dots.

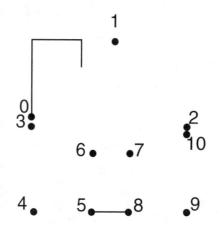

4. Draw lines to match.

two　　　one　　　five　　　seven　　　ten

0　1　2　3　4　5　6　7　8　9　10

six　　zero　　nine　　four　　eight　　three

14

Name	**Date**

Number of Players: 2 to 4

Materials

- a copy of a Bunny Board for each player (see bottom of page)

- a 10-sided spinner (located on the next page)

- 10 counters for each player (pennies, plastic chips, etc.)

How to Play: Take turns spinning the spinner. When it stops, say the number aloud and put a counter on the bunny with that number. If the number has already been covered, you miss the turn. The first person to cover all ten bunnies is the winner.

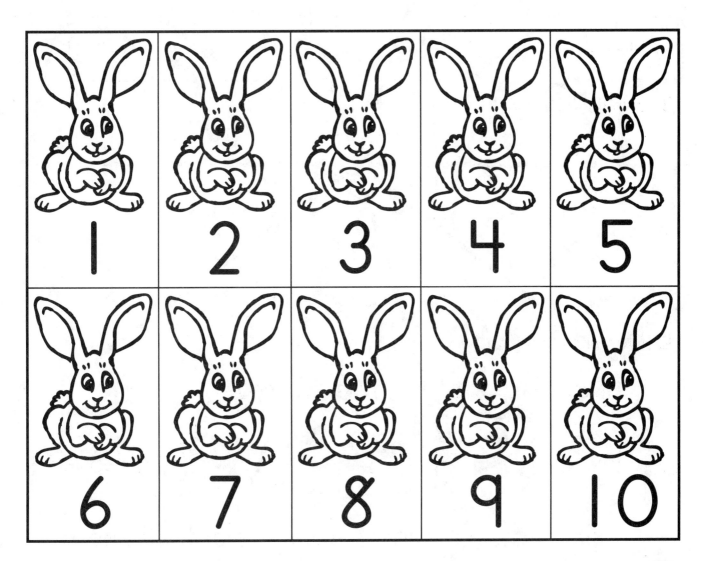

Name	**Date**

Color and cut out the spinner. Put a paper clip over the tip of the pencil on the center of the spinner and spin the paper clip.

NUMBERS TO 20

Unit 2

Ordinals
Before, after, between
Estimation
Counting by twos

Objectives

- uses appropriate mathematical language
- understands ordinals and their sequence
- uses and recognizes the ordinal names from 1st to 10th
- says number names/numerals to 20 in correct sequence
- counts forwards and backwards by 1s from any number in range 0–20
- recognizes numeral names zero to ten
- makes groups of up to ten objects
- makes groups of given size
- recognizes numerals from 0–20
- orders groups according to the number of objects
- counts in 2s
- uses language of odd and even

Language

number, numeral, ordinal, symbol, one, two, three, four, five, six, seven, eight, nine, ten, eleven, twelve, thirteen, fourteen, fifteen, sixteen, seventeen, eighteen, nineteen, twenty, first, second, third, fourth, fifth, sixth, seventh, eighth, ninth, tenth, eleventh, twelfth, thirteenth, fourteenth, fifteenth, sixteenth, seventeenth, eighteenth, nineteenth, twentieth, last, before, after, between, forwards, backwards, estimate, tallying, tally mark, even, odd

Materials/Resources

sharp pencil, colored pencils, sharp left/right handed scissors, glue, blank paper

Contents of Student Pages

* Materials needed for each reproducible student page

Page 19 Ordinal Numbers
position; drawing lines to match the ordinal symbol to the ordinal word; following directions for ordinals

* colored pencils

Page 20 More Ordinal Numbers
following directions; using ordinal language

* colored pencils

Page 21 After, Before, Between
writing the numeral in the correct position

Page 22 Estimating
estimating and then accurately checking by counting; recording results as a tally mark

Page 23 Join and Count the Numbers
counting backwards; filling the missing numerals

Page 24 Order the Sets
counting sets from zero to twenty in the correct sequence; writing the numerals; writing the missing numbers in sequence; odd and even

* scissors, glue, blank paper

Page 25 Assessment

Remember

❑ Before starting, each student is able to refer to resources in the classroom to form numerals correctly and to aid in counting (Example: number charts to 20).

❑ Before starting, each student is encouraged to use a ruler to draw lines.

Additional Activities

- ❑ *Chant counting to 20 forwards, backwards, and in twos and fives. Count as many items as possible, such as colored pencils in containers, counters, corks, stones, etc.*

- ❑ *Find, cut out, and glue on spare paper, pictures in magazines of large quantities of houses, pieces of fruit, or people. Make this a competition between pairs or groups of children. Say, "Who can be the first to complete sets from 11 to 20?"*

- ❑ *Sing extended songs to include the numbers to 20 such as "Ten Little Indians."*

- ❑ *Refer to wall charts for the formation of numerals and counting.*

- ❑ *Play board games such as Number Bingo, etc. Encourage the students to design their own board game. Set them in different environments (e.g., under the sea or in space). Use the themes from the class as a base for a game (e.g., "Help the spider reach the center of the web" or "Get Captain Cook out to Australia."*

- ❑ *Practice forming the numbers correctly by tracing and copying.*

Answers

Page 19 Ordinal Numbers

1. Check to make sure the first car is red, the second car is blue, the third car is green, the fourth car is orange, the fifth car is yellow, and the sixth car is brown.

2. fifth = 5th, second = 2nd, sixth = 6th, fourth = 4th, first = 1st, third = 3rd, ninth = 9th, eighth = 8th, seventh = 7th, tenth = 10th

3. Check to make sure the cat is in first place, the dog is in second place, and the snake is in third place.

Page 20 More Ordinal Numbers

1. Check to make sure the first snail is red, the second snail has brown spots, the third snail has pink dots, the fourth snail is blue, the fifth snail is orange, sixth snail has yellow stripes, the seventh snail has a gray dot, the eighth snail has a black zigzag, the ninth snail is purple, and the tenth snail is green.

2.

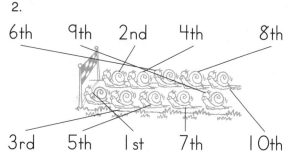

Page 21 After, Before, Between

1. 4, 8, 10, 1, 6
2. 2, 6, 8, 4
3. 4, 9, 7, 5
4. after, between, before, after

Page 22 Estimating

1.–6. Answers will vary.
7. a. 13
   b. 12
   c. 16
   d. 18
   e. 20
   f. 17

Page 23 Join and Count the Numbers

1.

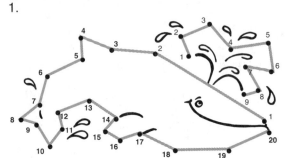

I am a whale.

2. 19, 18, 16, 15, 14, 13, 11
   10, 8, 7, 5, 4, 2, 1

Page 24 Order the Sets

Smallest to Largest: box with nothing in it, 2 elephants, 4 dogs, 6 rabbits, 8 raccoons, 10 koala bears, 12 quail, 14 fish, 16 mice, 18 apes, 20 worms

Numerals: 0, 2, 4, 6, 8, 10, 12, 14, 16, 18, 20

Missing Numbers: 1, 3, 5, 7, 9, 11, 13, 15, 17, 19

Page 25 Assessment

1. 15 dogs, 9 elephants
2. Check to make sure 20 triangles are drawn in a line and colored correctly.
3. a. 13, 18, 10, 16, 19, 12, 14
   b. 18, 12, 15, 11, 13, 19, 16
   c. 16, 13, 19, 14, 18
4.

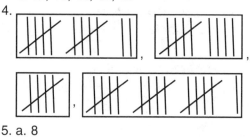

5. a. 8
   b. 10
   c. 16
   d. 20
   e. 13
   f. 19

Name   **Date**

1. Color the 1st car red.

Color the 2nd car blue.

Color the 3rd car green.

Color the 4th car orange.

Color the 5th car yellow.

Color the 6th car brown.

2. Draw a line from each word to the matching ordinal number.

fifth   second   sixth   fourth   first

9th   3rd   8th   2nd   5th   1st   4th   6th   10th   7th

third   ninth   eighth   seventh   tenth

3. Draw a cat in the first place at the pet show.
Draw a dog in second place at the pet show.
Draw a snake in third place at the pet show.

```
              ┌──────────┐
              │    1     │
    ┌─────────┘          └─────────┐
    │    2    │          │    3     │
    └─────────┴──────────┴──────────┘
```

(19)

| **Name** | **Date** |

1. **a.** Color the first snail red.

   b. Color the fourth snail blue.

   c. Color the ninth snail purple.

   d. Give the second snail brown spots.

   e. Give the sixth snail yellow stripes.

   f. Put pink dots on the third snail.

   g. Draw a black zigzag on the eighth snail.

   h. Color the fifth snail orange.

   i. On the seventh snail draw a gray dot.

   j. Make the tenth snail green.

2. Draw lines to match the snail to its place.

6th   9th   2nd   4th   8th

3rd   5th   1st   7th   10th

Name	Date

1. Which number comes **after** the one shown?

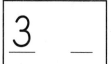   

| 3 __ | 7 __ | 9 __ | 0 __ | 5 __ |

2. Which number comes **before** the one shown?

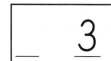 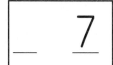 

| __ 3 | __ 7 | __ 9 | __ 5 |

3. Which number comes **between** the two shown?

| 3 __ 5 | 8 __ 10 | 6 __ 8 | 4 __ 6 |

4. Is the dark number **before**, **after**, or **between**?

| 4 **5** | 2 **3** 4 | 9 **10** | 7 **8** |

_____ _____ _____ _____

      #8989 Targeting Math: Numeration and Fractions

Name	Date

 one   ‖ two   ⫼ three   ⫼⫼ four   卌 five

1. How many boys are in the class?

   I think about [ ]

   Draw a tally mark for each one. = [   ]

2. How many girls are in the class?

   I think about [ ]

   Draw a tally mark for each one. = [   ]

3. How many windows are in the room?

   I think about [ ]

   Draw a tally mark for each one. = [   ]

4. Count the doors, and cupboard doors, in the room.   I think about [ ]

   Draw a tally mark for each one. = [   ]

5. How many red pencils can you find?

   I think about [ ]

   Draw a tally mark for each one. = [   ]

6. How many teachers are there in the school?   I think about [ ]

   Draw a tally mark for each one. = [   ]

7.

   a. 卌 卌 ⫼ = [ ]   b. 卌 卌 ‖ = [ ]

   c. 卌 卌 卌 | = [ ]   d. 卌 卌 卌 ⫼ = [ ]

   e. 卌 卌 卌 卌 = [ ]   f.  卌 卌 卌 ‖ = [ ]

#8989 *Targeting Math: Numeration and Fractions*

Name	**Date**

1. Join the dots from **1** to **20**. Then join the dots from **1** to **9**.

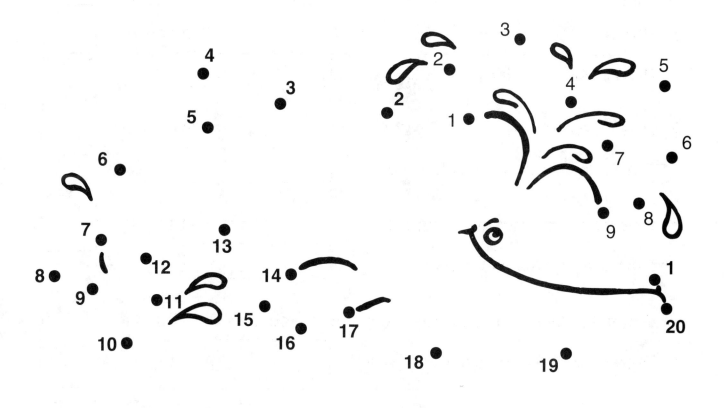

I am a _____.

2. Fill in the missing numbers by counting backwards.

20			17				12	
	9			6			3	

23

Name   **Date**

Cut out each set and glue it on a piece of paper in the correct sequence from smallest to largest. Write the numeral under each set. They are all **even** numbers. Now, on a separate sheet of paper, write the missing numbers from smallest to largest. They are **odd** numbers.

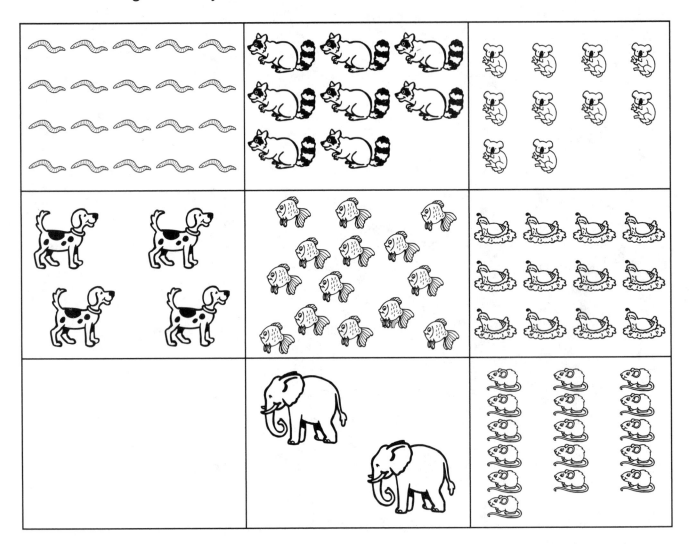

Name	**Date**

1. How many?

 =

=

2. Draw twenty triangles in a line.

Color the fifth green, the 12th yellow, the triangle before the 16th red, the triangle after the 10th orange, put purple spots on the seventeenth, and draw stripes on the first and last.

3. **a.** Write the numeral that comes **before** the one shown

___, 14 | ___, 19 | ___, 11 | ___, 17 | ___, 20 | ___, 13 | ___, 15

b. Write the numeral that comes **after** the one shown

17, ___ | 11, ___ | 14, ___ | 10, ___ | 12, ___ | 18, ___ | 15, ___

c. Write the numeral which comes **between** the ones shown.

15, ___, 17 | 12, ___, 14 | 18, ___, 20 | 13, ___, 15 | 17, ___, 19

4. Draw tally marks for the following amounts.

12 [ ]   9 [ ]   5 [ ]   16 [ ]

5. **a.**  = [ ]   **b.** = [ ]

c. = [ ]   **d.** = [ ]

e.  = [ ]   **f.** = [ ]

25

MORE NUMERATION

The focus of these two units is on numbers up to and including 100. Skills used include patterning, counting forwards and backwards, and writing numbers in numerals and words using a calculator with two-digit numbers. There are exercises counting by twos, fives, and tens. Filling in numerals on a hundreds chart, drawing tens and ones, completing a dot-to-dot picture and making up joining-number activities all reinforce the knowledge of numbers to one hundred. There is some calculator work. Two assessment pages and the activity page, which is a word hunt, help to further reinforce the concept of larger numbers.

#8989 Targeting Math: Numeration and Fractions

NUMBERS TO 100

Unit 1

Sequencing
Numerals and words
Missing numbers

Objectives

- counts forwards up to 20 and 100
- answers mathematical questions using pictures and imagery
- counts forwards and backwards starting from any whole number
- orders and represents whole numbers up to 100
- names and records numbers up to 100
- uses number skills involving whole numbers to solve problems

Language

how many, hundreds chart, hundreds place, numbers, numbers to 100, numerals, ones, ones place, place value, shorts, "teen," tens, tens and ones, tens place

Materials/Resources

colored pencils, blank paper, playing cards, timer, hundreds chart, plasticine, environmental materials, unifix cubes, Base 10 materials, blocks, painting materials (optional)

Contents of Student Pages

* Materials needed for each reproducible student page

Page 30 Numbers 11–19
labeling pictures with numerals; drawing pictures of corresponding numerals; coloring pictures according to numerals

* colored pencils

Page 31 How Many?
writing numerals; matching numerals and word numbers; counting by ones forwards and backwards

Page 32 Numbers to 20
dot-to-dot picture; coloring by number

* colored pencils

Page 33 Practice to 100
filling in missing numbers on a hundred chart; writing numbers as words; writing numerals

Page 34 Dot-to-Dot to 100
dot-to-dot picture; joining the dots to 100

* colored pencils

Page 35 Numbers 20–99
writing tens and ones as numerals; matching word numbers, numerals and tens and ones

Page 36 Assessment
* colored pencils

Page 37 Word Hunt Activity

Remember

- ❏ Use a variety of vocabulary when discussing numbers to 100.
- ❏ Explain the meaning of "teen."
- ❏ Explain place value of numbers going from right to left (i.e., units/ones, tens, hundreds).
- ❏ Refer to a hundreds chart whenever possible.

Additional Activities

❏ *Write down numbers up to 20 forwards or backwards as fast as the student can. Time them. Beat the time!*

❏ *Repeat the above activity writing numbers to 100.*

❏ *Students make up their own dot-to-dot pictures either to 20 or 100. Give them to a friend to complete.*

❏ *Students write stories about different numbers. Illustrate the stories.*

❏ *Memory/Concentration (pairs, small groups)— Write numerals up to 20 or 100 onto cards and their expanded notation or word form onto other cards. Place them face down. The aim is to find pairs of numerals and expanded notation or word forms. Winner is the person with the most pairs.*

❏ *A student picks a number between 0 and 20 or 0 and 100. The student says "higher" or "lower" until his or her partner guesses the correct number. The winner is the person who needs the least amount of guesses to work out the missing number. (Use hundreds chart if necessary, for help.)*

❏ *Students make 3-D numbers using blocks, plasticine, environmental materials, unifix cubes, etc.*

❏ *Students paint different numerals.*

Answers

Page 30 Numbers 11–19

1. a. 15
   b. 12
   c. 11
   d. 17
2. a. Check to make sure there are 13 trees drawn.
   b. Check to make sure there are 18 suns drawn.
   c. Check to make sure there are 15 hats drawn.
3. a. Check to make sure there are 11 balls colored.
   b. Check to make sure there are 14 candles colored.

Page 31 How Many?

1. a. 20
   b. 11
   c. 13
   d. 19
   e. 15
   f. 17
2. ten and nine =19; seventeen = 17; fourteen = 14; eighteen = 18; twenty = 20; ten and one = 11; twelve = 12; ten and six = 16
3. a. 13, 14
   b. 13, 16, 18
   c. 14, 17, 18
   d. 13, 14, 16, 17

4. a. 19, 17
   b. 16, 14, 13
   c. 16, 13, 12
   d. 16, 15, 14

Page 32 Numbers to 20

1. Make sure picture is colored.

2. Check to make sure numbers are colored appropriately.

Page 33 Practice to 100

1.

1	2	3	4	5	6	7	8	9	10
11	**12**	13	**14**	**15**	16	**17**	**18**	19	**20**
21	**22**	**23**	24	**25**	**26**	**27**	28	**29**	30
31	32	33	**34**	**35**	**36**	37	**38**	**39**	**40**
41	**42**	**43**	**44**	45	46	**47**	**48**	49	**50**
51	**52**	**53**	54	**55**	**56**	**57**	58	**59**	60
61	62	**63**	**64**	**65**	**66**	67	**68**	**69**	**70**
71	**72**	73	**74**	**75**	76	**77**	**78**	79	**80**
81	**82**	**83**	**84**	85	**86**	**87**	**88**	**89**	90
91	**92**	**93**	94	**95**	**96**	**97**	98	**99**	**100**

2. a. twenty-three
   b. forty
   c. sixty-five
   d. thirty-one
   e. seventy-two
   f. fifty-nine
   g. eighty-nine
   h. forty-four
3. a. 27
   b. 40
   c. 93
   d. 35
   e. 78
   f. 66
   g. 51
   h. 80

Answers (cont.)

Page 34 Dot-to-Dot to 100

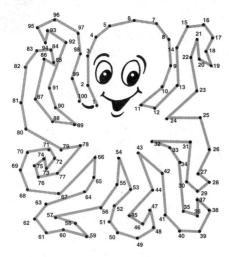

Page 35 Numbers 20–99

1. a. 50
   b. 43
   c. 97
   d. 80
2. 62, sixty-two, 6 tens 2 ones
   91, ninety-one, 9 tens 1 one
   55, fifty-five, 5 tens 5 ones
   44, forty-four, 4 tens 4 ones
   34, thirty-four, 3 tens 4 ones
3. a. 6 tens 4 ones = 64
   b. 3 tens 7 ones = 37
   c. 5 tens 0 ones = 50
   d. 9 tens 9 ones = 99

Page 36 Assessment

1. a. Check to make sure 12 snakes are drawn.
   b. Check to make sure 17 hats are drawn.
2. ten and five, 15, fifteen
   ten and two, 12, twelve
   ten and nine, 19, nineteen
   ten and ten, 20, twenty
3. a. 14, 16, 18
   b. 19, 17, 15, 14
   c. 16, 17, 18, 20
   d. 16, 14, 13, 11
4. a. fifty-two
   b. seventy-four
   c. twenty-eight
   d. forty
5. a. 73
   b. 89
   c. 41
   d. 60
6. Make sure blocks are colored.
   a. 56
   b. 82

Page 37 Word Hunt Activity

E	F	T	W	E	C	S	E	V	L	E	W	T
L	I	N	H	T	E	N	I	A	N	A	L	W
E	V	E	L	R	C	I	O	X	U	N	T	O
V	E	S	F	E	N	E	E	T	X	I	S
E	T	T	E	O	N	E	T	F	O	Y	O	D
N	W	R	V	U	E	N	I	Y	T	T	E	E
I	E	I	E	R	E	F	T	F	H	H	Y	R
N	N	H	N	N	T	N	I	G	14	T	F	D
E	T	T	T	E	E	F	I	U	R	O	N	N
T	Y	X	E	V	N	E	D	I	R	R	E	U
Y	I	N	E	E	I	G	H	T	E	E	N	H
S	D	S	N	S	N	T	Y	T	H	G	I	E

Secret Message: WE CAN ALL COUNT TO ONE HUNDRED

Name	**Date**

1. How many are there?

a.  _____

b.  _____

c.  _____

d.  _____

2. Draw:

  a. 13 trees.

  b. 18 suns.

  c. 15 hats.

3. Color:

  a. eleven balls.

  b. fourteen candles.

Name	Date

1. Write these numbers.

Example: ten and seven   _17_

a. ten and ten   ____   **b.** ten and one   ____

c. ten and three   ____   **d.** ten and nine   ____

e. ten and five   ____   **f.** ten and seven   ____

2. Match each number with its name.

ten and nine

17

fourteen

14

twenty

19

twelve

12

16   seventeen

11   eighteen

20   ten and one

18   ten and six

3. Complete.

Example: 10, 11, _12_, _13_, 14, 15

a. 11, 12, ____, ____, 15, 16   **b.** ____, 14, 15, ____, 17, ____

c. ____, 15, 16, ____, ____, 19   **d.** 12, ____, ____, 15, ____, ____

4. Complete.

a.

20		18		16	15

b.

18	17		15		

c.

	15	14			11

d.

17				13	12

31

Name	Date

1. Complete the dot-to-dot picture. Color it.

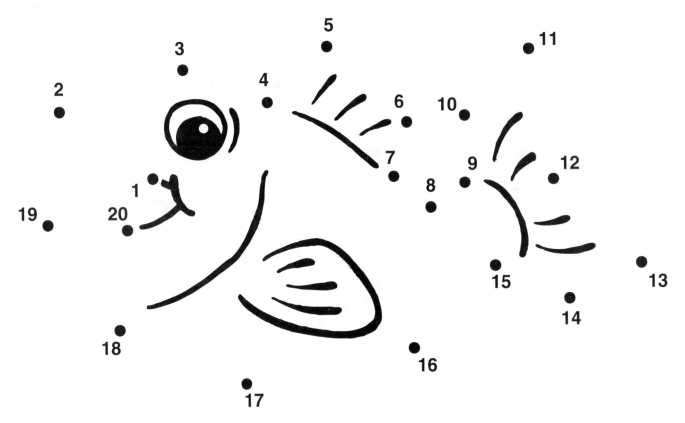

2. Color the numbers using the code below.

CODE

eleven (yellow)

fourteen (dark blue)

fifteen (red)

seventeen (dark green)

eighteen (orange)

twenty (light green)

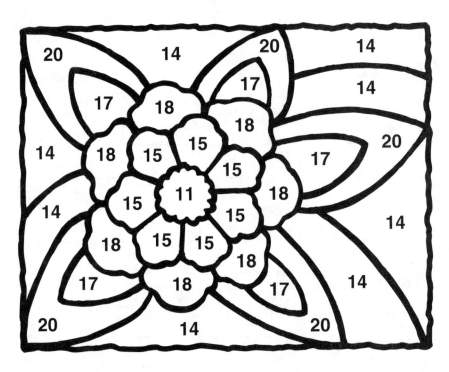

#8989 Targeting Math: Numeration and Fractions

Name	Date

1. Fill in the missing numbers.

1	2			5		7			10
		13			16			19	
21			24				28		30
	32	33				37			
41				45	46			49	
			54				58		60
	62					67			
71		73			76			79	
				85					90
			94				98		

2. Write the numbers in words.

a. 23 _____

b. 40 _____

c. 65 _____

d. 31 _____

e. 72 _____

f. 59 _____

g. 89 _____

h. 44 _____

3. Write these numerals.

a. twenty-seven _____

b. forty _____

c. ninety-three _____

d. thirty-five _____

e. seventy-eight _____

f. sixty-six _____

g. fifty-one _____

h. eighty _____

Name	Date

Complete the dot-to-dot picture. Color it.

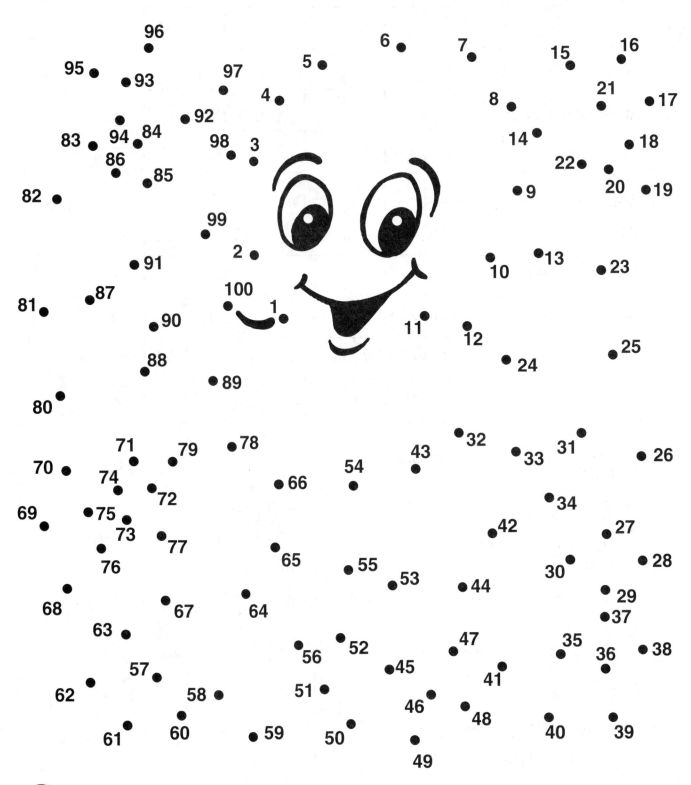

Name	**Date**

1. Complete.

Example: 3 tens 6 ones = <u>36</u>

a. 5 tens and 0 ones = _____   **b.** 4 tens 3 ones = _____

c. 9 tens 7 ones = _____   **d.** 8 tens 0 ones = _____

2. Match these. One has been done for you.

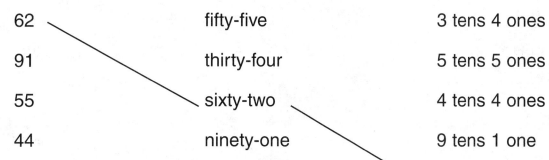

62	fifty-five	3 tens 4 ones
91	thirty-four	5 tens 5 ones
55	sixty-two	4 tens 4 ones
44	ninety-one	9 tens 1 one
34	forty-four	6 tens 2 ones

3. Complete.

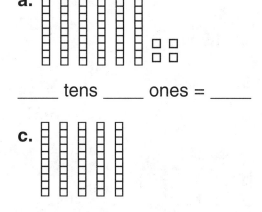

a. _____ tens _____ ones = _____

b. _____ tens _____ ones = _____

c. _____ tens _____ ones = _____

d. _____ tens _____ ones = _____

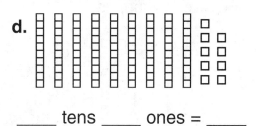

35

Name	**Date**

1. Draw:

   a. 12 snakes.   **b.** 17 hats.

2. Match.

ten and five	19	twenty
ten and two	20	twelve
ten and nine	15	nineteen
ten and ten	12	fifteen

3. Complete.

   a. 13, ____, 15, ____, 17, ____   **b.** ____, 18, ____, 16, ____, ____

   c. 15, ____, ____, ____, 19, ____   **d.** ____, 15, ____, ____, 12, ____

4. Write these numbers in words.

   a. 52 _____   **b.** 74 _____

   c. 28 _____   **d.** 40 _____

5. Write these numerals.

   a. seventy-three   _____   **b.** eighty-nine   _____

   c. forty-one   _____   **d.** sixty   _____

6. Color and complete.

   a.   **b.**

   5 tens 6 ones = _____   8 tens 2 ones = _____

36

Name   **Date**

E	F	T	W	E	C	S	E	V	L	E	W	T
L	I	N	H	T	E	N	I	A	N	A	L	W
E	V	E	L	R	C	I	O	X	U	N	T	O
V	E	E	S	F	E	N	E	E	T	X	I	S
E	T	T	E	O	N	E	T	F	O	Y	O	D
N	W	R	V	U	E	N	I	Y	T	T	E	E
I	E	I	E	R	E	F	T	F	H	H	Y	R
N	N	H	N	N	T	N	I	G	14	T	F	D
E	T	T	T	E	E	F	I	U	R	O	N	N
T	Y	X	E	V	N	E	D	I	R	R	E	U
Y	I	N	E	E	I	G	H	T	E	E	N	H
S	D	S	N	S	N	T	Y	T	H	G	I	E

All of these words are in the puzzle above. One of them is written in numerals. The words may be horizontal, vertical, or diagonal. They may also be forwards or backwards. Circle the letters as you find each word. Sometimes a letter is used in more than one word.

ONE	SEVEN	THIRTEEN	NINETEEN	SEVENTY
TWO	EIGHT	FOURTEEN	TWENTY	EIGHTY
THREE	NINE	FIFTEEN	THIRTY	NINETY
FOUR	TEN	SIXTEEN	FORTY	HUNDRED
FIVE	ELEVEN	SEVENTEEN	FIFTY	
SIX	TWELVE	EIGHTEEN	SIXTY	

Write the secret message from the unused letters starting from the top and going left to right. _____

37

MORE NUMBERS TO 100

Unit 2

Counting by 10s
Counting by 2s
Counting by 5s
Counting forwards and backwards
Using a calculator

Objectives

- ❑ obtains and tests rules to continue number sequences
- ❑ counts by ones, twos, fives, and tens, both forwards and backwards up to 100 starting from any number
- ❑ orders whole numbers by counting forwards and backwards up to 100
- ❑ estimates and calculates mentally, including adding and subtracting 10
- ❑ recognizes patterns in lines of a hundreds chart
- ❑ uses a calculator to explore basic mathematical concepts
- ❑ identifies, continues, and invents whole number patterns

Language

even, how many, hundreds chart, multiples, number lines, numbers, numbers to 100, numerals, numeration, odd, ones, patterns, place value, tens, whole numbers

Materials/Resources

writing/drawing/painting materials, blank paper, playing cards, timer, hundreds chart, calculators

Contents of Student Pages

* Materials needed for each reproducible student page

Page 40 Patterns

counting by ones, twos and fives both forwards and backwards; cross out number which does not belong; join numbers counting by fives and twos

Page 41 Counting by Tens

using whole numbers; counting forwards and backwards

Page 42 Counting by Twos

completing hundreds chart and answer questions; counting forwards and backwards

* colored pencils

Page 43 Counting by Fives

counting forwards and backwards; filling in missing numbers on hundreds chart; answering questions about hundreds chart

* colored pencils

Page 44 Counting by Tens

using different starting points; counting forwards and backwards; complete number lines

Page 45 Calculator Activities

adding numbers starting at 0; adding and subtracting numbers starting at 0

* calculators

Page 46 Assessment

* calculators

Remember

- ❑ Explain the word "numeration."
- ❑ Review place value of numbers going from right to left (i.e., units/ones, tens, hundreds).
- ❑ Encourage students to refer to a hundreds chart whenever possible.

Additional Activities

❑ *Have students write numbers up to 100 forwards or backwards as fast as the they can. Time them. Have them try and beat their own time.*

❑ *Students draw or write stories about different numbers. Have them illustrate the stories.*

❑ *A student picks a number between 0 and 100. The student says "higher" or "lower" until his or her partner guesses the correct number. The winner is the person who needs the least amount of guesses to work out the missing number. (Use hundreds chart, if necessary, for help.)*

❑ *Have students find little words in the word "Numeration."*

❑ *Have students paint patterns of numbers.*

❑ *Have students list and draw where numbers are used in the environment.*

Answers

Page 40 Patterns

1. a. 23, 24, 25
   b. 59, 60, 61
   c. 85, 84, 83
   d. 50, 55, 60
   e. 75, 70, 65
   f. 36, 38, 40

2. a. 27
   b. 67
   c. 89
   d. 35
   e. 62
   f. 76

3.

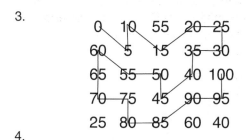

4.

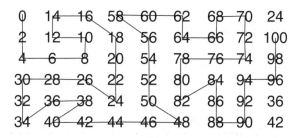

Page 41 Counting by Tens

1. a. 50, 70
   b. 30, 50, 70, 80
   c. 20, 30, 40, 50, 70
   d. 30, 40, 60, 70, 80

2. a. 70, 50
   b. 70, 60, 40 20
   c. 90, 70, 50, 40
   d. 60, 40, 30, 20, 0

3. a. 20, 30, 50, 60, 70
   b. 30, 50, 60, 70, 90, 100
   c. 90, 80, 60, 50, 30

Page 42 Counting by Twos

1. a. 2, 4, 6, 8, 10
      12, 14, 16, 18, 20
      22, 24, 26, 28, 30

32, 34, 36, 38, 40
42, 44, 46, 48, 50
52, 54, 56, 58, 60
62, 64, 66, 68, 70
72, 74, 76, 78, 80
82, 84, 86, 88, 90
92, 94, 96, 98, 100

   b. Make sure all even numbers are colored.
   c. even

2. a. 36, 40, 46
   b. 24, 28, 32, 34
   c. 76, 74, 70, 66
   d. 98, 94, 90, 86, 84
   e. 50, 56, 58, 62, 64

Page 43 Counting by Fives

1. a. 20, 30
   b. 30, 35, 45
   c. 60, 65, 80
   d. 35, 40, 55, 65

2. a. 70, 60, 50
   b. 95, 90, 80, 70
   c. 35, 30, 20, 15, 5
   d. 70, 65, 50, 40, 35

3. a.

1	**2**	3	**4**	**5**	6	**7**	**8**	9	**10**
11	**12**	**13**	14	**15**	**16**	17	**18**	**19**	**20**
21	22	**23**	**24**	25	**26**	**27**	28	**29**	30
31	**32**	33	**34**	**35**	36	**37**	**38**	39	**40**
41	**42**	**43**	44	**45**	**46**	47	**48**	**49**	50
51	52	**53**	**54**	55	**56**	**57**	58	**59**	**60**
61	**62**	63	**64**	**65**	66	**67**	**68**	69	**70**
71	**72**	**73**	74	**75**	**76**	77	**78**	**79**	80
81	82	**83**	**84**	85	**86**	**87**	**88**	**89**	**90**
91	**92**	93	**94**	**95**	96	**97**	98	**99**	**100**

   b. Make sure all multiples of 5 are colored.
   c. The numbers either have a 5 or 0 at the end.

Page 44 Counting by Tens

1. a. 53, 23
   b. 45, 75, 85
   c. 21, 31, 51
   d. 77, 67, 47, 37

2. a. 58, 38, 18
   b. 22, 32, 62, 72, 92
   c. 64, 54, 34, 24, 4
   d. 6, 26, 36, 56, 66
   e. 79, 59, 49, 29, 19

Page 45 Calculator Activities

1. a. 3, 6, 9, 12, 15
   b. 2, 4, 6, 8, 10
   c. 1, 2, 3, 4, 5
   d. 4, 8, 12, 16, 20

2. a. 50, 70, 40, 20, 70
   b. 90, 60, 70, 0, 30
   c. 80, 60, 74, 23, 74
   d. 70, 20, 32, 12, 53

3. a. 49
   b. 56
   c. 69
   d. 42

Page 46 Assessment

1. a. 82, 88, 90
   b. 51, 53, 55
   c. 77, 75, 71
   d. 90, 84, 82, 80

2. a. 20, 30, 35, 45
   b. 95, 85, 80, 70, 65, 55
   c. 45, 50, 55, 65, 70, 75, 80
   d. 40, 30, 25, 20, 10, 5

3. a. 10, 40, 50, 70, 80
   b. 90, 80, 60, 50, 40
   c. 31, 41, 51, 71, 91

4. a. 80
   b. 43
   c. 62
   d. 45

Name	**Date**

1. Complete.

   (Example: 13, 14, 15, _16_ , _17_ , _18_)

   a. 20, 21, 22, ___ , ___ , ___   **b.** 56, 57, 58, ___ , ___ , ___

   c. 88, 87, 86, ___ , ___ , ___   **d.** 35, 40, 45, ___ , ___ , ___

   e. 90, 85, 80, ___ , ___ , ___   **f.** 30, 32, 34, ___ , ___ , ___

2. Cross out the number that does **not** belong.

   (Example: 2, 4, 6, ✗, 8, 10)

   a. 15, 20, 25, 27, 30   **b.** 66, 67, 68, 70, 72   **c.** 100, 99, 89, 98, 97

   d. 20, 30, 35, 40, 50   **e.** 57, 58, 59, 60, 62   **f.** 76, 75, 70, 65, 60

3. Join the numbers to count by fives to 100.

0	10	55	20	25
60	5	15	35	30
65	55	50	40	100
70	75	45	90	95
25	80	85	60	40

4. Join the numbers to count by twos to 100.

0	14	16	58	60	62	68	70	24
2	12	10	18	56	64	66	72	100
4	6	8	20	54	78	76	74	98
30	28	26	22	52	80	84	94	96
32	36	38	24	50	82	86	92	36
34	40	42	44	46	48	88	90	42

(40)

Name	**Date**

1. Complete.

a.

10	20	30	40		60		80	

b.

	40		60			90	100

c.

0	10				60	

d.

20			50				90	

2. Fill in the missing numbers.

a. 100   90   80   60   40

b. 80   50   30

c.   80   60   30

d.   50   10

3. Complete.

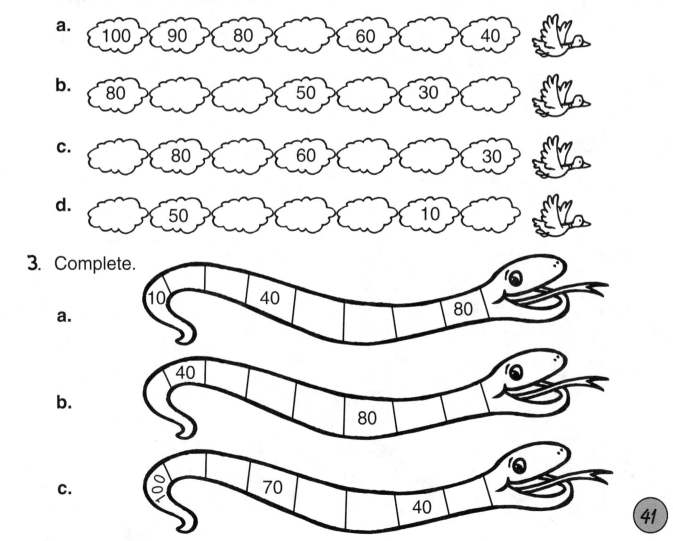

a. 10   40   80

b. 40   80

c. 100   70   40

Name								Date	

1. **a.** Fill in the missing numbers.

1		3		5		7		9	
11		13		15		17		19	
21		23		25		27		29	
31		33		35		37		39	
41		43		45		47		49	
51		53		55		57		59	
61		63		65		67		69	
71		73		75		77		79	
81		83		85		87		89	
91		93		95		97		99	

b. Color in the numbers you wrote.

c. Are the colored numbers **odd** or **even**? _____

2. Complete.

a.

32	34		38		42	44		48

b.

20	22		26		30			36

c.

80	78			72		68		64

d.

100		96		92		88		

e.

	52	54			60			66

42

Name	**Date**

1. Complete.

   a. 5, 10, 15, ____, 25, ____, 35   **b.** 20, 25, ____, ____, 40, ____, 50

   c. 55, ____, ____, 70, 75, ____   **d.** ____, ____, 45, 50, ____, 60, ____

2. Complete.

a.

85	80	75		65		55	

b.

100			85		75		65

c.

		25			10		0

d.

		60	55		45		

3. **a.** Fill in the missing numbers.

1		3			6			9	10
11			14			17			
	22			25			28		30
		33			36			39	
41			44			47			50
	52			55			58		
		63			66			69	
71			74			77			80
	82			85					
		93			96		98		

   b. Color in the multiples of 5.

   c. What pattern do you see?_____

   _____

(43)

Name **Date**

1. Complete.

a.
73
63
43
33

b.
55
65
95

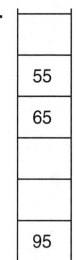

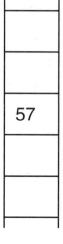

c.
11
41
61

d.
87
57

2. Complete these number lines.

a.
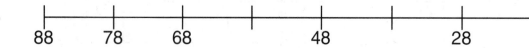
88   78   68   48   28

b.
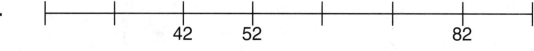
42   52   82

c.

74   44   14

d.
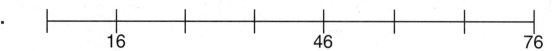
16   46   76

e.

89   69   39

44

Name	**Date**

1. Use a calculator to find these answers.

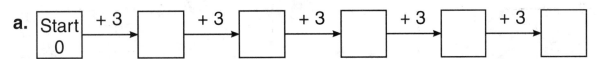

a. Start 0 → + 3 → ☐ → + 3 → ☐ → + 3 → ☐ → + 3 → ☐ → + 3 → ☐

b. Start 0 → + 2 → ☐ → + 2 → ☐ → + 2 → ☐ → + 2 → ☐ → + 2 → ☐

c. Start 0 → + 1 → ☐ → + 1 → ☐ → + 1 → ☐ → + 1 → ☐ → + 1 → ☐

d. Start 0 → + 4 → ☐ → + 4 → ☐ → + 4 → ☐ → + 4 → ☐ → + 4 → ☐

2. Find these answers using a calculator.

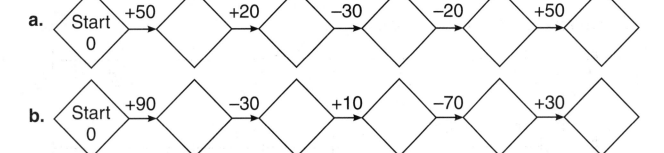

a. Start 0 → +50 → ◇ → +20 → ◇ → −30 → ◇ → −20 → ◇ → +50 → ◇

b. Start 0 → +90 → ◇ → −30 → ◇ → +10 → ◇ → −70 → ◇ → +30 → ◇

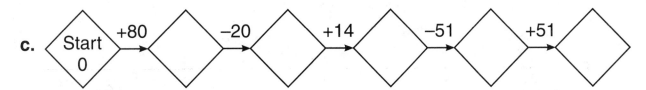

c. Start 0 → +80 → ◇ → −20 → ◇ → +14 → ◇ → −51 → ◇ → +51 → ◇

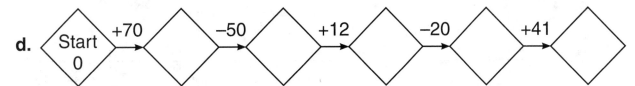

d. Start 0 → +70 → ◇ → −50 → ◇ → +12 → ◇ → −20 → ◇ → +41 → ◇

3. Complete using a calculator.

   a. 21 + 30 + 40 − 57 + 15 = _____   **b.** 60 − 23 + 33 − 14 = _____

   c. 100 − 92 + 48 + 29 − 16 = _____   **d.** 73 − 37 + 15 − 9 = _____

45

Name	Date

1. Count by twos and complete.

   a. 80, _____, 84, 86, _____, _____　　　　**b.** 45, 47, 49, _____, _____, _____

   c. 79, _____, _____, 73, _____, 69　　　**d.** _____, 88, 86, _____, _____, _____

2. Count by fives and complete.

   a.

   15　　　　25　　　　　　　　40　　　50　　55

   b.
   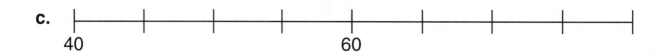
   90　　　　　　　75　　　　　　60

   c.
   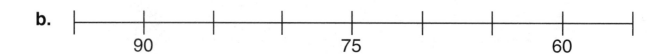
   40　　　　　　　60

   d.

   35　　　　　　　15　　　　　　0

3. Count by tens and complete.

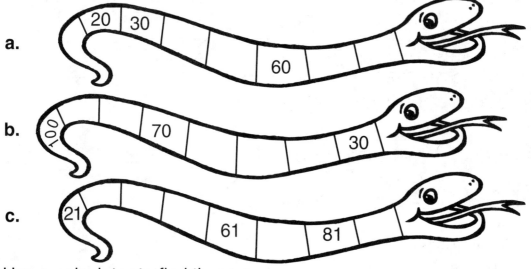

   a. 20 | 30 | | | 60

   b. 100 | | 70 | | | | 30

   c. 21 | | | 61 | | 81

4. Use a calculator to find these answers.

   a. $33 + 33 - 22 + 45 - 9 = $ _____　　　　**b.** $100 - 38 - 26 + 7 = $ _____

   ⟨46⟩ **c.** $80 - 20 - 35 + 37 - 0 = $ _____　　　**d.** $99 - 66 - 33 + 45 = $ _____

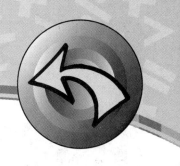

EVEN MORE NUMERATION

These two units focus on numbers up to and including 1,000. Concepts are reinforced with many varied activities. These include using Base 10 materials to model numbers and recognizing numbers from Base 10 models. Numbers are also modeled on an abacus. Further practice is gained by ordering numbers, counting in hundreds, estimating the size of large groups, using given digits to make large and small numbers and spending money. The activity page is a game that uses a calculator and three-digit numbers to progress along the game board. There are two assessment pages.

NUMBERS TO 1,000

Unit 1

**Recognizing
Estimating
Counting groups
Matching words/
    numerals
Ordering numerals**

Objectives

• orders whole numbers up to 999

• makes, names, records, and renames numbers up to 999

• counts forwards and backwards up to 1,000 in 1s, 10s and 100s starting from any whole number

• estimates the size of larger collections by grouping the items

• selects and carries out the operation appropriate to situations involving addition or subtraction

• counts, compares, and orders whole numbers up to 999 and represents them in symbols and words stating the place value of any digit

• uses materials and models to develop part-whole understanding of numbers

• demonstrates an understanding that numbers can be represented using groupings of 10, 100, and 1,000

• uses number skills involving whole numbers to solve problems

Language

match, number, 101–999, one hundred and one-nine hundred and ninety-nine, groups of 10, actual, estimate, count, total, groups, more, join, hundreds, tens, same, cheapest, dearest

Materials/Resources

colored pencils, Base 10 materials, scissors, glue, spare paper, dice, calculators, counters, (optional: dough or clay, craft sticks, blank cards)

Contents of Student Pages

* Materials needed for each reproducible student page

Page 50 Words/Numerals
recognizing numerals; matching numerals in everyday situations

* colored pencils

Page 51 Estimating
estimating groups; estimating and checking by counting in groups of 10 and 100; drawing a group of more than 100

* colored pencils

Page 52 Counting in Hundreds
matching group, word, and numeral; dot to dot in 100s

* colored pencils, Base 10 materials, spare paper

Page 53 Hundreds
recognizing and coloring groups of Base 10 materials; writing number words and numerals

* colored pencils

Page 54 Models
recognizing models; writing groups in terms of hundreds, tens, ones; coloring to represent groups

* colored pencils

Page 55 Money
ordering numbers within groups of 100

* colored pencils, scissors, glue

Page 56 Assessment
* colored pencils

Page 57 Game Activity
using a calculator with three-digit numbers

* counters, dice, calculators

Remember

❏ In order for students to perform operations with three-digit numbers, they need a strong understanding of place value.

❏ When doing student pages, discuss with students how bus routes are read, (e.g., "670" is not "six hundred and seventy").

Additional Activities

❏ *Give students opportunities to build models of three-digit numbers using concrete materials.*

❏ *Students bring details of numbers on license plates they have seen. Record and discuss numbers.*

❏ *Encourage students to share the numbers in their addresses. Have them bring the addresses in envelopes and discuss numbers.*

❏ *Play the game "Buzz" but count by 10s and buzz at 100.*

❏ *Students try to guess a number with you saying "more" or "less" until the correct number is chosen.*

❏ *What does 100 look like? As a class, make a "birthday cake" out of dough or clay. With students' help, put 100 craft sticks (candles) onto the cake.*

❏ *Write the words "one" to "nineteen," "one hundred" to "nine hundred" and "twenty" to "ninety" on cards. Make five lots of cards 0–10. Choose a student to say a three-digit number word (e.g., "eight hundred sixty-two"). Another student then has to find the cards to make the numeral 862. These cards can be used alternatively as an ordering game. Three students make a number word each. They then have to order the numbers.*

❏ *Discuss with students three-digit numbers that you come across in other key learning areas.*

Answers

Page 50 Words/Numerals

1. 144 = Mrs. L. Watkins, 414 = Mr. R. Thompson, 100 = Mr. R. Mooney, 1000 = Ms. L. Moyle
2. RV 325 = red, AAU 532 = yellow, NA 235 = blue, BAG 523 = green
3. 221 miles, 434 miles, 986 miles, 994 miles
4. BONDI = 670, CENTRAL = 870, ROCKDALE = 510, CITY = 410

Page 51 Estimating

1. a. Estimate = Answers will vary, Actual = 270
   b. Estimate = Answers will vary, Actual = 310
2. Estimate = Answers will vary, Actual = 189; draw 11 more houses

Page 52 Counting in Hundreds

1.

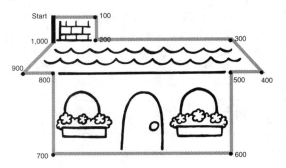

2. a. 4 hundred blocks = four hundred = 400
   b. 1 hundred block = one hundred = 100
   c. 7 hundred blocks = seven hundred = 700
   d. 10 hundred blocks = one thousand = 1,000

Page 53 Hundreds

1. One hundred is colored.
2. Six hundreds are colored.
3. Four hundreds are colored.
4. Nine hundreds are colored.
5. Five hundreds are colored.
6. Two hundreds are colored.
7. Eight hundreds are colored.
8. Ten hundreds are colored.

Page 54 Models

1. a. 8 hundreds, 0 tens, 0 ones = 800
   b. 4 hundreds, 6 tens, 5 ones = 465
   c. 6 hundreds, 4 tens, 8 ones = 648
   d. 6 hundreds, 3 tens, 0 ones = 630
   e. 7 hundreds, 1 ten, 1 one = 711
2. a. Three hundreds, two tens, and one one are colored.
   b. Five hundreds, four tens, and four ones are colored.
   c. Three hundreds, six tens, and five ones are colored.

Page 55 Money

1. $1–$99 = tricycle, $100–$199 = wheelbarrow, $200–$299 = desk, $300–$399 = bed, $400–$499 = entertainment unit, $500–$599 = stereo, $600–$699 = fridge, $700–$799 = table and chairs, $800–$899 = washing machine, $900–$999 = sofa
2. a. tricycle $39
   b. sofa $999

Page 56 Assessment

1. a. 6 hundreds, 3 tens, 5 ones = 635
   b. Five hundreds, five tens, two ones = 552
2. a. Six hundreds, one ten, and one one should be colored.
   b. Three hundreds, seven tens, and three ones should be colored.
3. a. 3
   b. 6
   c. 9
4. Estimate: Answers will vary. Actual: 254

Name	**Date**

1. Match each letter to the correct mailbox.

144   414   100   1000

Mr. R. Thompson 414 Holt Road Lipson, 56070	Mr. R. Mooney 100 Evatt Street Cotton Tree, 45581	Mrs. L. Watkins 144 Seaton Street Goulburn, 25802	Ms. L. Moyle 1000 Bell Road Fish Creek, 39593

2. Color the cars.

Blue = 235   Green = 523   Red = 325   Yellow = 532

RV 325   AAU 532   NA 235   BAG 523

3. These cars have been driven different distances. Look at the odometers and put them in order from shortest to the longest distance.

986	miles		434	miles		994	miles		221	miles

_____ _____ _____ _____

4. Help the driver put the correct signs on the buses.

BONDI   CENTRAL   ROCKDALE   CITY

CITY 410	BONDI 670	CENTRAL 870	ROCKDALE 510

50

Name	**Date**

1. Estimate the number in each group before counting to check. Group in tens.

   a.

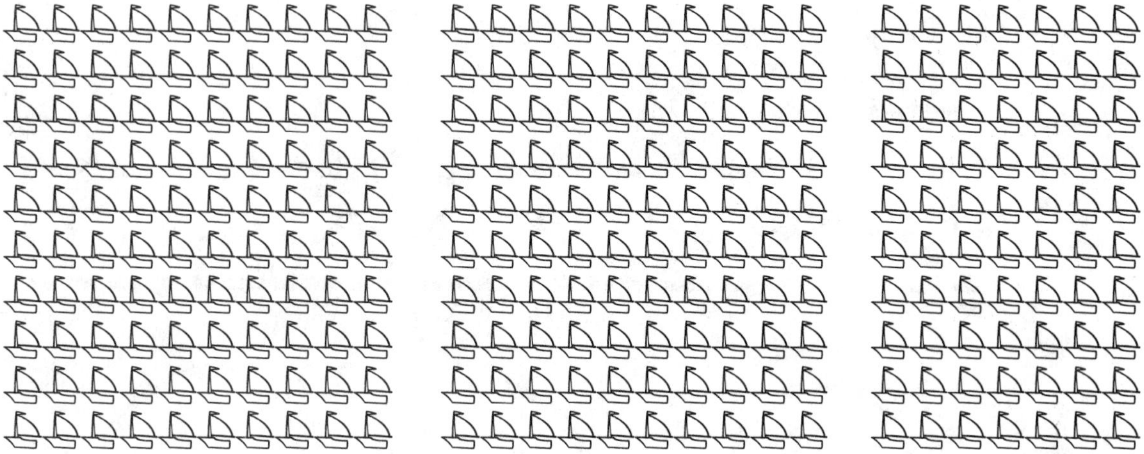

   Estimate _____   Actual _____

   b.

   Estimate _____   Actual _____

2. Estimate the number, then circle groups of 10 to check. Draw more houses to make the total 200.

   Estimate _____

   Actual _____

51

Name	Date

1. Join the dots to complete the picture, then color it.

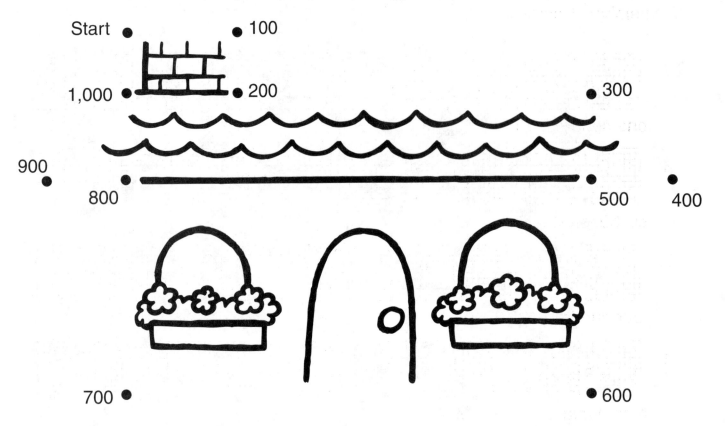

2. Use different colors to draw lines to match.

a.

one thousand

100

b.

seven hundred

400

c.

four hundred

1,000

d.

one hundred

700

Name	**Date**

Read the words and numerals and then color the correct number of blocks.
(Remember, 1 block = 100.)

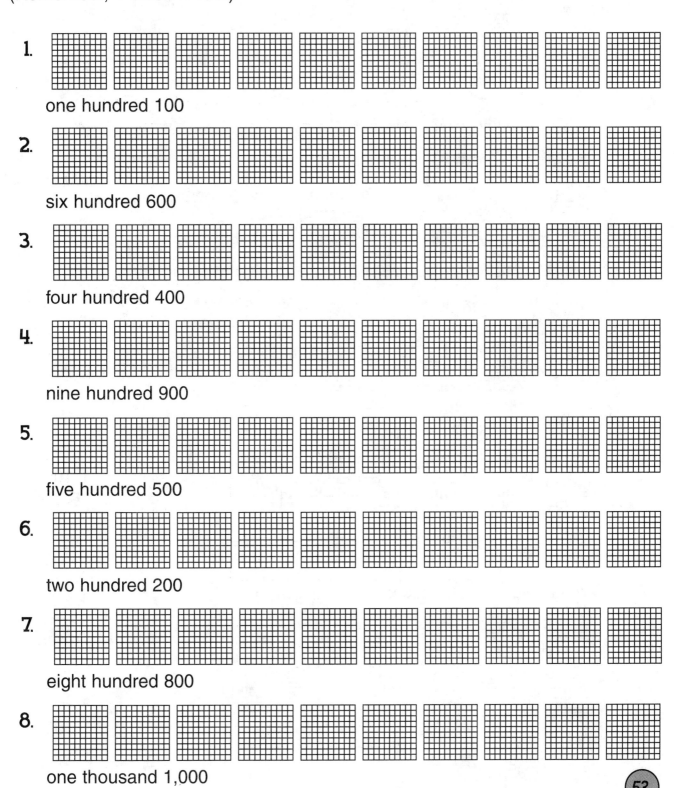

1.
one hundred 100

2.
six hundred 600

3.
four hundred 400

4.
nine hundred 900

5.
five hundred 500

6.
two hundred 200

7.
eight hundred 800

8.
one thousand 1,000

53

Name	Date

1. Write the numeral.

a.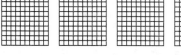

_____ hundreds   _____ tens   _____ ones = _____

b.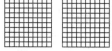

_____ hundreds   _____ tens   _____ ones = _____

c.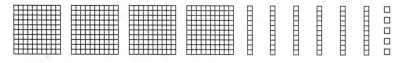

_____ hundreds   _____ tens   _____ ones = _____

d.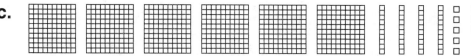

_____ hundreds   _____ tens   _____ ones = _____

e.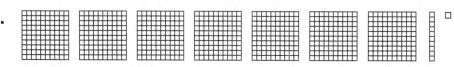

_____ hundreds   _____ tens   _____ one = _____

2. Color to make these numbers.

a. 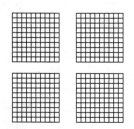 321

b. 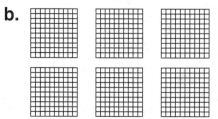 544

c. 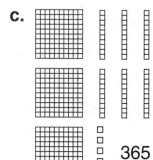 365

Name	Date

1. Help the shopkeeper place these items in the correct box. Color, then cut and paste them.

$1–$99	$100–$199	$200–$299	$300–$399	$400–$499

$500–$599	$600–$699	$700–$799	$800–$899	$900–$999

2. **a.** Which item is the least expensive? _____ How much? _____

   b. Which item is the most expensive? _____ How much? _____

Desk $279

Bed $399

Tricycle $39

Sofa $999

Washing machine $859

Fridge $699

Table and chairs $719

Entertainment unit $469

Wheelbarrow $109

Stereo $509

55

Name	**Date**

1. Write the numeral.

a. **b.**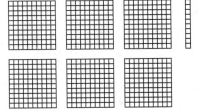

___ hundreds ___ tens ___ ones = _____   ___ hundreds ___ tens ___ ones = _____

2. Color the group to make these numbers.

a.  611

b.  373

3. Count the groups of 100.

a. 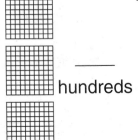 _____ hundreds

b. 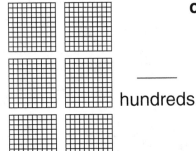 _____ hundreds

c. 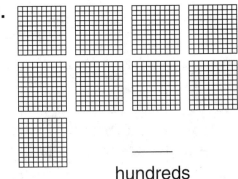 _____ hundreds

4. Estimate and then check by circling groups of 10.

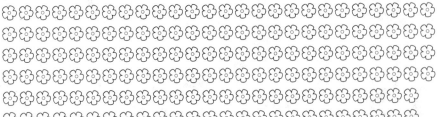

Estimate

_____

Actual

_____

#8989 Targeting Math: Numeration and Fractions   © *Teacher Created Resources, Inc.*

Name	Date

Number of Players

- 2–4

Materials

- an enlarged game board (below)
- a colored counter for each player
- a die
- a calculator for each player

How to Play

- Take turns rolling the die. Roll the die to see who goes first.
- Move forward the number of spaces shown on the die. When you land on a problem square, use the calculator to solve it. Move forward the number of spaces shown on the calculator. If you land on a star, go back 5 spaces.
- The first person to reach the calculator is the winner.

The game board (read in snaking order):

- Calculator (finish)
- 43
- 42 — ★
- 31
- 30 — $151 - 149 =$
- 19
- 18 — $79 - 75 =$
- 7
- 6

- 53
- 44 — $606 - 604 =$
- 41 — $118 - 116 =$
- 32 — ★
- 29
- 20 — $88 - 86 =$
- 17
- 8 — $101 - 97 =$
- 5

- 52 — $777 - 776 =$
- 45 — ★
- 40 — $555 - 549 =$
- 33 — $203 - 199 =$
- 28 — $171 - 168 =$
- 21 — $763 - 761 =$
- 16 — $142 - 136 =$
- 9
- 4 — $16 - 11 =$

- 51 — ★
- 46 — $300 - 294 =$
- 39
- 34 — $311 - 302 =$
- 27 — $201 - 196 =$
- 22
- 15
- 10 — ★
- 3

- 50 — $202 - 198 =$
- 47
- 38 — $416 - 415 =$
- 35
- 26
- 23 — $139 - 136 =$
- 14
- 11 — $18 - 14 =$
- 2 — $47 - 39 =$

- 49
- 48 — $818 - 815 =$
- 37 — ★
- 36 — $506 - 499 =$
- 25
- 24 — ★
- 13 — $25 - 19 =$
- 12
- 1 — Start

MORE NUMBERS TO 1,000

Unit 2

**Writing numerals
Number words
Number patterns
Calculator
Numeral expanders
Abacus
Place value**

Objectives

- uses materials and models to develop part-whole understanding of numbers
- counts, compares, and orders whole numbers up to 999 and represents them in symbols and words, stating the place value of any digit
- generates and represents repeating or simple counting number patterns
- counts forwards and backwards up to 1,000 in 1s, 10s, and 100s starting from any whole number
- uses a calculator to represent and explore numbers
- orders whole numbers to 999
- comments on information in displays produced by himself or herself and others
- sorts and describes objects in terms of their features, such as size and shape

Language

numerals, largest, smallest, model, one–nine, hundred, ninety, numbers, missing, number patterns, calculator, press, enter, more, less, mass, greatest, biggest, abacus, hundreds, tens, ones, numeral expander

Materials/Resources

Base 10 materials, calculators, colored pencils, abacus, (optional: dice, counters, grid paper)

Contents of Student Pages

* *Materials needed for each reproducible student page*

Page 61 Largest and Smallest
finding largest and smallest numbers from same three digits; writing numerals and number words

Page 62 Place Value
completing a hundreds/tens/ones chart; writing numerals for words; filling in missing numbers

Page 63 Exploring 500–600
using a calculator for exploring number patterns
* *calculator, colored pencils*

Page 64 Ordering Numbers
matching numerals by ordering according to size

Page 65 Abacus
recognizing numbers on an abacus; drawing abacus representations to match numeral; matching abacus representation and numeral
* *colored pencils*

Page 66 Numeral Expanders
reading numeral expanders; completing numeral expanders to state number in models; writing numbers for numeral expanders; writing numeral expanders for numbers

Page 67 Assessment

Remember

❏ Place value is critical in all strands of math, so it is vital that students have a thorough understanding of it.

© Teacher Created Resources, Inc.

Additional Activities

❑ Give students opportunities to build models of three-digit numbers on an abacus and to make numeral expanders.

❑ What does 1,000 look like? Encourage students to bring in similar sized small lids—counting them in groups of 10s, then 100s to reach 1,000. Stick them on thick cardboard and display. Count 1,000 of other suitable objects by dividing students into groups and getting each group to count 100.

❑ Students can play "change" in small groups, with one student in each group being the leader. The leader throws a die. The others have to decide to record the number thrown either in the hundreds, tens, or ones column. After three throws of the die, students see who created the biggest number. That student then becomes the leader.

❑ Play Bingo. Give students blank grid paper with 16 squares. Choose a group of numbers (Example: 500–515). Students write the numbers randomly in the squares. Call the numbers and show a number card as you say each number. When a student gets a line across or down, he or she calls out "Bingo." Students use counters, or mark with a symbol, each number counted.

❑ Play a variation of "I'm thinking of . . ." as a number game. Keep playing until someone suggests the correct number.

❑ Encourage students to bring empty plastic containers and food tins from home. Look at the numerals on them and discuss. Compare the sizes of the tins.

❑ Depending on students' interests, find references to three-digit numbers in the sporting pages and use them as a focus.

❑ Encourage students to bring catalogs from home showing three-digit prices. Discuss and display.

❑ Play a game of "The Price Is Right." Have students cut pictures out of catalogs (record prices elsewhere), and paste onto photo cards. Put out three cards (Examples: VCR, TV, and washing machine). Choose a student to put them in correct order of price (cheapest to the most expensive). Choose another student to estimate, then reveal prices and students see who was correct.

Answers

Page 61 Largest and Smallest

1. a. 981, 189
   b. 861, 168
   c. 987, 789
   d. 553, 355
   e. 642, 246
   f. 941, 149
   g. 632, 236
   h. 763, 367
   i. 710, 107
   j. 888, 888
2. a. eight hundred seventy-two
   b. four hundred fifty-one
   c. nine hundred eighty-six
   d. two hundred forty-four
   e. one hundred fifty-three
   f. seven hundred forty-seven
3. a. 696
   b. 422
   c. 855
   d. 387
   e. 933
   f. 207

Page 62 Place Value

1. a. 9, 5, 6
   b. 1, 2, 1
   c. 5, 3, 5
   d. 8, 4, 9
   e. 2, 9, 2
   f. 6, 6, 6
   g. 4, 4, 4
   h. 7, 8, 9
2. a. 380
   b. 964
   c. 529
   d. 893
   e. 902
   f. 199
3. a. 371, 374, 375
   b. 995, 996, 999
   c. 525, 527
   d. 158, 160
   e. 180, 190, 200
   f. 998, 996, 995
   g. 200, 400
   h. 700, 600
4. a. Answers will vary.
   b. Answers will vary.
   c. Answers will vary.

59

Answers (cont.)

Page 63 Exploring 500–600

1. a. 588
   b. 561
   c. 520
   d. 585
   e. 553
   f. 526
   g. 583
2. a. 504, 505, 506
   b. 540, 550, 560
   c. 597, 596, 595
   d. 535, 545, 555
3. a. The following numbers should be colored red: 510, 520, 530, 540, 550, 560, 570, 580, 590, 600
   b. The following numbers should marked with an X: 505, 510, 515, 520, 525, 530, 535, 540, 545, 560, 565, 570, 575, 580, 585, 590, 595, 600
4. a. The following numbers should be colored blue: 507, 510, 514, 512, 522, 530, 540, 535, 542, 552, 558, 568, 577

Page 64 Ordering Numbers

1. a. 220, 420, 110
   b. 140, 825, 425
   c. 420, 794
   d. 420, 110
   e. 110, 210
   f. 800, 400
2. a. The biggest can of peaches
   b. The smallest tins of baked beans, corn kernels, and tuna.
   c. The biggest tin of baked beans, the medium and biggest tins of peaches, the smallest and biggest tins of lentil soup, the biggest can of corn kernels, and the biggest can of whole tomatoes.

Page 65 Abacus

1. a. 462
   b. 869
   c. 752
   d. 991
   e. 308
   f. 830
2. a. Four hundreds, two tens, and seven ones should be drawn.
   b. Nine hundreds, eight tens, and three ones should be drawn.
   c. Five hundreds, six tens, and six ones should be drawn.
3. a. Should match 836
   b. Should match 399
   c. Should match 500
   d. Should match 145
   e. Should match 940
   f. Should match 711

Page 66 Numeral Expanders

1. a. 4, 9, 8, 498
   b. 6, 6, 2, 662
   c. 2, 6, 3, 263
   d. 5, 4, 4, 544
   e. 8, 2, 5, 825
2. a. 536
   b. 864
   c. 273
   d. 681
3. a. 9, 9, 9
   b. 6, 3, 4
   c. 2, 5, 6
   d. 8, 7, 3
   e. 1, 3, 8
   f. 5, 8, 1

Page 67 Assessment

1. a. 254
   b. 686
   c. 442
   d. 810
2. a. 9, 6, 4
   b. 6, 8, 2
   c. 3, 4, 9
   d. 2, 9, 5
3. a. 149, 151, 153
   b. 414, 415, 416
   c. 198, 196, 195
   d. 861, 863, 864
4. 4, 3, 9, 10, 1, 5, 7, 6, 2, 8
5. a. 876
   b. 151
   c. 372
6. a. 853
   b. 390
7. a. 7, 3, 7
   b. 1, 7, 3

60

Name	**Date**

1. Rearrange the numerals to form the largest and smallest numbers possible.

Numerals	Largest number	Smallest number	Numerals	Largest number	Smallest number
a. 9, 1, 8			**b.** 8, 1, 6		
c. 7, 9, 8			**d.** 5, 5, 3		
e. 2, 4, 6			**f.** 4, 9, 1		
g. 6, 3, 2			**h.** 7, 6, 3		
i. 1, 7, 0			**j.** 8, 8, 8		

2. Write each number in words. You may need to use some of these words to help you.

> one, two, three, four, five, six, seven, eight, nine, ten, eleven, twelve, thirteen, fourteen, fifteen, sixteen, seventeen, eighteen, nineteen, twenty, thirty, forty, fifty, sixty, seventy, eighty, ninety, hundred

a. | 872 | _____

b. | 451 | _____

c. | 986 | _____

d. | 244 | _____

e. | 153 | _____

f. | 747 | _____

3. Write the numeral for each of these.

a. six hundred ninety-six

b. four hundred twenty-two

c. eight hundred fifty-five

d. three hundred eighty-seven

e. nine hundred thirty-three

f. two hundred seven

Name	Date

1. Write these numbers on the chart.

   a. nine hundred fifty-six
   b. one hundred twenty-one
   c. five hundred thirty-five
   d. eight hundred forty-nine
   e. two hundred ninety-two
   f. six hundred sixty-six
   g. four hundred forty-four
   h. seven hundred eighty-nine

Hundreds	Tens	Ones

2. Write the numerals.

   a. three hundreds and eight tens   _____
   b. nine hundreds, six tens, and four ones   _____
   c. five hundreds, two tens, and nine ones   _____
   d. eight hundreds, nine tens, and three ones   _____
   e. nine hundreds and two ones   _____
   f. one hundred, nine tens, and nine ones   _____

3. Fill in the missing numbers.

   a. ____, 372, 373, ____ , ____
   b. ____ , ____ , 997, 998, ____
   c. 524, ____ , 526, ____ , 528
   d. 156, 157, ____ , 159, ____
   e. 160, 170, ____ , ____ , ____
   f. 999, ____ , 997, ____ , ____
   g. 100, ____ , 300, ____ , 500
   h. 900, 800, ____ , ____ , 500

4. Do some missing number puzzles for a friend to solve.

   a. _____, _____, _____, _____, _____, _____

   b. _____, _____, _____, _____, _____, _____

   c. _____, _____, _____, _____, _____, _____

Name	**Date**

1.

501	502	503	504	505	506	507	508	509	510
511	512	513	514	515	516	517	518	519	520
521	522	523	524	525	526	527	528	529	530
531	532	533	534	535	536	537	538	539	540
541	542	543	544	545	546	547	548	549	550
551	552	553	554	555	556	557	558	559	560
561	562	563	564	565	566	567	568	569	670
571	572	573	574	575	576	577	578	579	580
581	582	583	584	585	586	587	588	589	590
591	592	593	594	595	596	597	598	599	600

a. What number is one more than 587? _____

b. What number is one less than 562? _____

c. What number is ten more than 510? _____

d. What number is ten less than 595? _____

e. What number is two more than 551? _____

f. What number is three more than 523? _____

g. What number is three less than 586? _____

2. Complete these patterns.

a. 501, 502, 503, _____, _____, _____

b. 510, 520, 530, _____, _____, _____

c. 600, 599, 598, _____, _____, _____

d. 505, 515, 525, _____, _____, _____

3. Use a calculator.

501	502	503	504	505	506	507	508	509	510
511	512	513	514	515	516	517	518	519	520
521	522	523	524	525	526	527	528	529	530
531	532	533	534	535	536	537	538	539	540
541	542	543	544	545	546	547	548	549	550
551	552	553	554	555	556	557	558	559	560
561	562	563	564	565	566	567	568	569	670
571	572	573	574	575	576	577	578	579	580
581	582	583	584	585	586	587	588	589	590
591	592	593	594	595	596	597	598	599	600

a. Color 510 red and enter 510 on the calculator. Enter [+] [10] [=] and color [520] red. Keep pressing [+] [10] [=]. Color each total red.

b. Put an X on 505 and enter 505 on the calculator. Enter [+] [5] [=] and put an X on 510. Keep pressing [+] [5] [=]. Put an X on each total.

4. Use a calculator.

501	502	503	504	505	506	507	508	509	510
511	512	513	514	515	516	517	518	519	520
521	522	523	524	525	526	527	528	529	530
531	532	533	534	535	536	537	538	539	540
541	542	543	544	545	546	547	548	549	550
551	552	553	554	555	556	557	558	559	560
561	562	563	564	565	566	567	568	569	670
571	572	573	574	575	576	577	578	579	580
581	582	583	584	585	586	587	588	589	590
591	592	593	594	595	596	597	598	599	600

a. Enter 501, Press [+] [6] [=] and color the answer blue. You should be on [507]. Follow these instructions and color each total blue.

[+] [3] [=],	[+] [4] [=],	[−] [2] [=]
[+] [10] [=],	[+] [8] [=],	[+] [10] [=]
[−] [5] [=],	[+] [7] [=],	[+] [10] [=]
[+] [6] [=],	[+] [10] [=],	[+] [9] [=]

(63)

Name	**Date**

1. Write the correct volume on each can.

a.

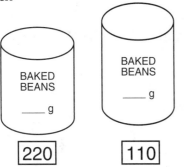

220	110	420

b.

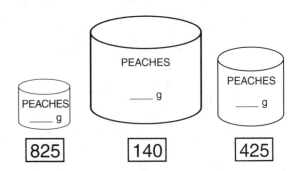

825	140	425

c.

420
794

d.

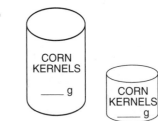

110
420

e.

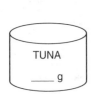

110
210

f.

400
800

2. **a.** Which can has the greatest volume?

_____

b. Which cans have the smallest volume?

_____

c. Which cans have a volume of 420 g or more?

_____

#8989 Targeting Math: Numeration and Fractions

Name	**Date**

1. Write the numerals.

a.

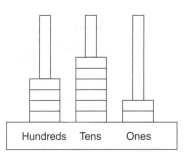

b.

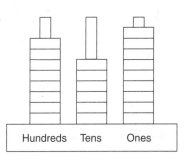

c.

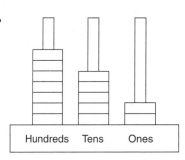

d.

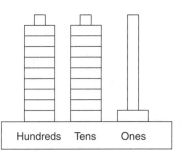

e.

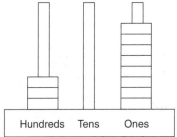

f.

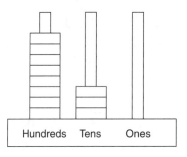

2. Show these numbers on the abacus.

a.

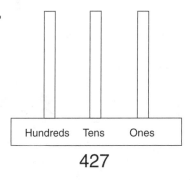

427

b.

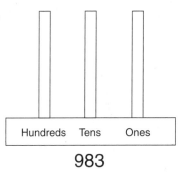

983

c.

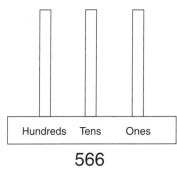

566

3. Color the abacus and its number to match.

a.

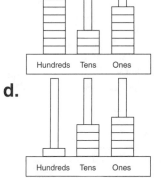

b.

c.

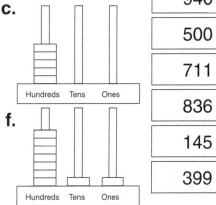

d.

e.

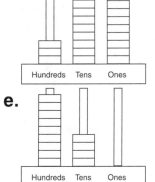

f.

940
500
711
836
145
399

65

Name	**Date**

1. Complete the numeral expander and fill in the boxes.

Example: **a.**   **b.**

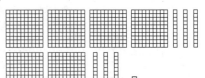
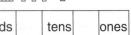

7	hundreds	3	tens	5	ones

hundreds	tens	ones

hundreds	tens	ones

735

c.   **d.**   **e.**

hundreds	tens	ones

hundreds	tens	ones

hundreds	tens	ones

2. Write the number for each numeral expander.

a.
5	hundreds	3	tens	6	ones

b.
8	hundreds	6	tens	4	ones

c.
2	hundreds	7	tens	3	ones

d.
6	hundreds	8	tens	1	ones

3. Complete the numeral expander for these numbers.

a.
999

	hundreds		tens		ones

b.
634

	hundreds		tens		ones

c.
256

	hundreds		tens		ones

d.
873

	hundreds		tens		ones

e.
138

	hundreds		tens		ones

f.
581

	hundreds		tens		ones

Name	**Date**

1. Write the number.

   a. two hundred fifty-four   _____

   b. six hundred eighty-six   _____

   c. four hundred forty-two   _____

   d. eight hundred ten   _____

2. Write these numbers on the chart.

Hundreds	Tens	Ones

   a. nine hundreds, six tens, and four ones

   b. six hundreds, eight tens, and two ones

   c. three hundreds, four tens, and nine ones

   d. two hundreds, nine tens, and five ones

3. Fill in the missing numbers.

   a. ____, 150, ____ , 152, ____   **b.** 413, ____, ____, ____, 417

   c. 199, ____, 197, ____, ____   **d.** 860, ____, 862, ____, ____

4. Order these numbers from smallest to biggest using the numbers 1–10.

421	370	900	998	115	525	763	634	251	814

5. Write the numerals for the numbers shown on the abacus.

   a. 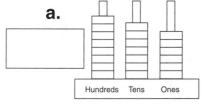   **b.** 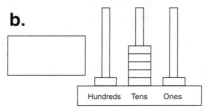   **c.**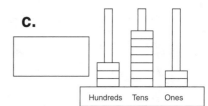

6. Write the number.

   a. 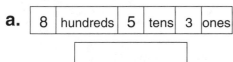   **b.**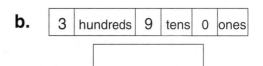

7. Fill in the numeral expanders.

   a. 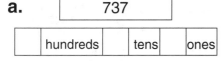   **b.**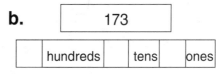

           #8989 Targeting Math: Numeration and Fractions

CALCULATORS AND ESTIMATION

The Calculator Unit concentrates on key recognition, using the correct keys, and making calculator sentences. Simple algorithms are solved and number sentences are written to solve problems. Patterning is practiced using colors, a hundreds chart, and the calculator. There are three fun activities where the calculator is used in an investigative way. There is also an assessment page.

The Estimation Unit investigates estimating measurements as well as numbers. Area, height, and length are estimated using informal units. How many in a group and the answer to problems are estimated before actual answers are worked out. An assessment page is included.

CALCULATORS

Unit 1

Addition
Subtraction
Using correct keys
Reading displays

Objectives

- accurately presses a given sequence of buttons on a calculator
- uses available technology to explore mathematical concepts
- uses available technology to help in the solution of mathematical problems
- represents numbers in a variety of forms, including with the use of a calculator
- recognizes what works and what did not work while answering mathematical questions
- writes complete number sentences using one of the +, −, and = signs
- uses a calculator to represent and explore numbers, place value, and operations
- uses a calculator to record numbers and to explore counting sequences
- approximates, counts, compares, orders, and represents whole numbers and groups of objects up to 100

Language

press, numbers, sign, calculator, display panel, equal, keys, add totals, all clear, biggest number, smallest number, groups, number sentence, pattern, subtract, target

Materials/Resources

calculators, pencils, colored pencils, spare paper, scissors, glue, dice

Contents of Student Pages

* *Materials needed for each reproducible student page*

Remember

- ❏ Regularly check to see if students are using correct operations.
- ❏ Remind students of the function of the key that clears the calculator.

Additional Activities

- ❏ *Provide students with many opportunities to understand basic operations using calculators (with teacher guidance).*

- ❏ *Encourage students in groups and in pairs to communicate their observations and findings through talking, writing, and drawing.*

- ❏ *Provide opportunities for free exploration with calculators. Get students to share their findings.*

- ❏ *Use calculators when possible in other areas (e.g., science).*

- ❏ *Give students supermarket catalogs. Have them cut out what they want to buy, paste it on paper, and use the calculator to find the total amount spent.*

- ❏ *Encourage students to make up math stories with the use of calculators.*

- ❏ *Provide opportunities for students to find that calculators can talk (e.g., 2 x 4 + 6 turned upside down reads "hi"). Have a wall chart where students can write their ideas for others to try.*

- ❏ *Calculator Game—This game is played with two players and with one, two or three dice (depends on level). Each student takes a turn to throw the dice. The first die represents the tens (hundreds) the other ones (tens). The student keys in the number and keeps a cumulative total. The highest total at the end is the winner.*

- ❏ *Give beginners calculator activities that involve reading digital numbers (e.g., construct digital numerals using craft sticks).*

- ❏ *Provide opportunities for students to check algorithm answers.*

- ❏ *Provide opportunities for students to find how many ways they can find a particular number using a calculator.*

- ❏ *Give students combinations of numbers and see what are the largest and smallest answers they can find.*

Answers

Page 72 Correct Keys
1. 4
2. 7
3. 4
4. 9
5. 3
6. 9

Page 73 Addition
1. a. 5, 3 + 2 = 5
   b. 4, 2 + 2 = 4
   c. 10, 6 + 4 = 10
   d. Answers will vary.
2. a. 9
   b. 14
   c. 14
   d. 11
   e. 15
   f. 11
3. a. Answers will vary.
   b. Answers will vary.
   c. Answers will vary.
   d. Answers will vary.

Page 74 Addition and Subtraction
1. 1 + 2 = 3, 1 + 3 = 4, 4 + 3 = 7, 5 + 1 = 6, 2 + 4 = 6, 10 − 3 = 7, 2 + 2 = 4, 6 − 3 = 3, 5 − 2 = 3, 10 − 6 = 4, 1 + 4 = 5, 6 − 2 = 4, 7 − 3 = 4, 6 − 1 = 5, 9 − 5 = 4, 1 + 1 = 2
2. 1 + 2 = 3 (purple), 1 + 3 = 4 (blue), 4 + 3 = 7 (green), 5 + 1 = 6 (yellow), 2 + 4 = 6 (yellow), 10 − 3 = 7 (green), 2 + 2 = 4 (blue), 6 − 3 = 3 (purple), 5 − 2 = 3 (purple), 10 − 6 = 4 (blue), 1 + 4 = 5 (red), 6 − 2 = 4 (blue), 7 − 3 = 4 (blue), 6 − 1 = 5 (red), 9 − 5 = 4 (blue), 1 + 1 = 2 (orange)

Page 75 Calculator Sentences
Answers will vary.

Page 76 Calculator Flowers

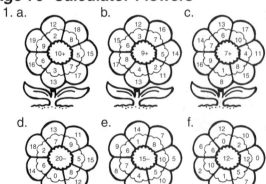

1. a. b. c. d. e. f.

2. Answers will vary.

Answers *(cont.)*

Page 77 More Calculators

1. The following numbers should be colored red: 3, 6, 9, 12, 15, 18, 21, 24, 27, 30, 33, 36, 39, 42, 45, 48, 51, 54, 57, 60, 63, 66, 69, 72, 75, 78, 81, 84, 87, 90, 93, 96, 99
2. The following numbers should be colored blue: 10, 20, 30, 40, 50, 60, 70, 80, 90, 100
3. Answers will vary.

Page 78 Assessment

1. a. 7
   b. 9
   c. 5
   d. 8
   e. 2
   f. 1
   g. 5
   h. 7
   i. 4
   j. 19
   k. 4
   l. 38
   m. 70
   n. 91
   o. 98
   p. 57
   q. 12
   r. 36
2. a. 45 − 30 = 15
   b. 27 + 32 = 59
3.

a.   b.   c.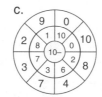

4. Answers in the chart will vary. The smallest number is 0 and the largest number is 7.

Page 79 Calculator Shapes Activity

1.–3. Teacher to check.

Page 80 Calculator Words Activity

1. a. sob
   b. hog
   c. leg
   d. big
   e. she
   f. eel
   g. sell
   h. hose
   i. zoos
   j. oboe
   k. bible
   l. sizzle
   m. shells
   n. gobble
2. a.–j. Answers will vary.

Page 81 Broken Keys Activity

1.–4. Answers will vary.

Name	**Date**

Press these numbers and signs into a calculator. Write the number shown in the display panel.

1. | 3 | + | 1 | = |

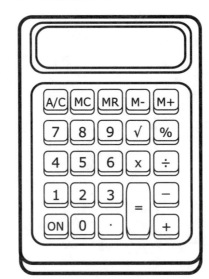

2. | 4 | + | 3 | = |

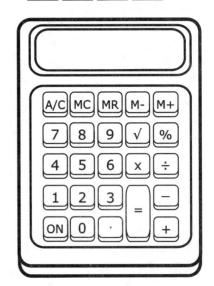

3. | 2 | + | 2 | = |

4. | 5 | + | 4 | = |

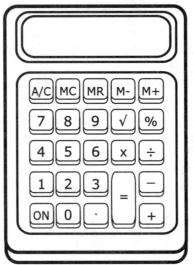

5. | 0 | + | 3 | = |

6. | 6 | + | 3 | = |

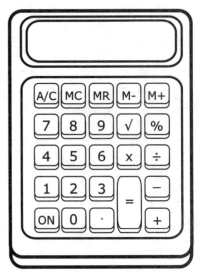

Name **Date**

1. Press each number sentence into the calculator to find the total. Press the clear button after each one.

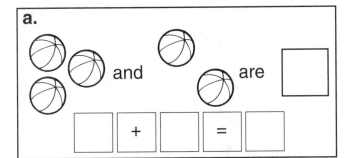

a.

and are ☐

☐ + ☐ = ☐

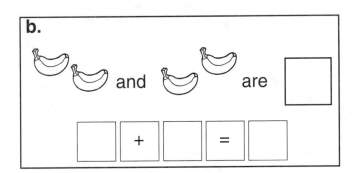

b.

and are ☐

☐ + ☐ = ☐

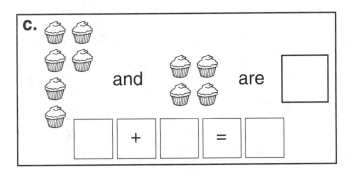

c.

and are ☐

☐ + ☐ = ☐

d. Do one yourself.

and are ☐

☐ + ☐ = ☐

2. Key these numbers into a calculator to find totals. Don't forget to press the clear button after each one.

a. 4 + 5 = ☐

b. 7 + 7 = ☐

c. 6 + 8 = ☐

d. 9 + 2 = ☐

e. 5 + 10 = ☐

f. 2 + 9 = ☐

3. Now you can try some of your own.

a. ☐ + ☐ = ☐

b. ☐ + ☐ = ☐

c. ☐ + ☐ = ☐

d. ☐ + ☐ = ☐

#8989 Targeting Math: Numeration and Fractions

Name	**Date**

1. Use the calculator to complete these number sentences.

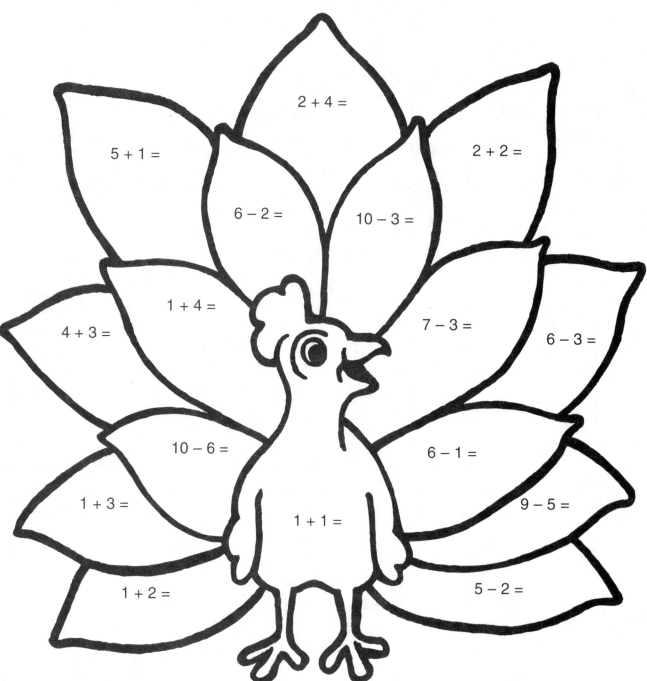

2. Color the feathers.

2 is Orange	3 is Purple	4 is Blue
5 is Red	6 is Yellow	7 is Green

#8989 Targeting Math: Numeration and Fractions

Name	**Date**

Use a calculator to find a number sentence for each leg. Use the

numbers   1 2 3 4 5 and the keys + − .

Name   **Date**

1. Fill in the petals.

a.   b.   c.

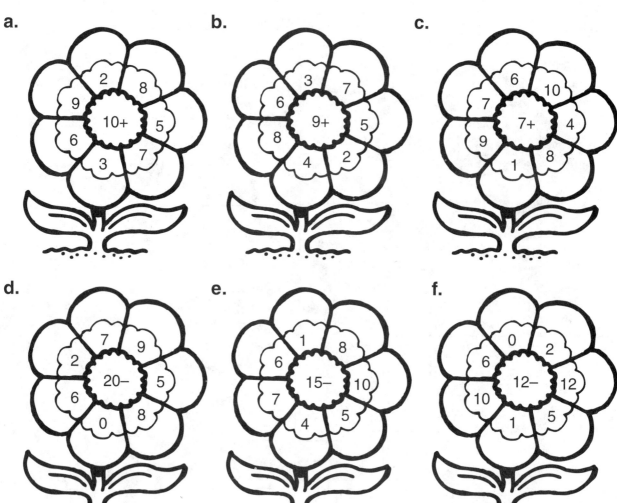

d.   e.   f.

2. Make your own flowers and find the answers using the calculator.

| **Name** | **Date** |

1. Color 3 red. Press 3 on a calculator.

   Enter + 3 , color 6 red.

   Keep pressing + 3 .

   Color each total red.

1	2	3	4	5	6	7	8	9	10
11	12	13	14	15	16	17	18	19	20
21	22	23	24	25	26	27	28	92	30
31	32	33	34	35	36	37	38	39	40
41	42	43	44	45	46	47	48	49	50
51	52	53	54	55	56	57	58	59	60
61	62	63	64	65	66	67	68	69	70
71	72	73	74	75	76	77	78	79	80
81	82	83	84	85	86	87	88	89	90
91	92	93	94	95	96	97	98	99	100

2. Color 10 blue. Press 10 on a calculator.

   Enter + 10 , color 20 blue.

   Keep pressing + 10 .

   Color each total blue.

1	2	3	4	5	6	7	8	9	10
11	12	13	14	15	16	17	18	19	20
21	22	23	24	25	26	27	28	92	30
31	32	33	34	35	36	37	38	39	40
41	42	43	44	45	46	47	48	49	50
51	52	53	54	55	56	57	58	59	60
61	62	63	64	65	66	67	68	69	70
71	72	73	74	75	76	77	78	79	80
81	82	83	84	85	86	87	88	89	90
91	92	93	94	95	96	97	98	99	100

3. Create your own problem.

1	2	3	4	5	6	7	8	9	10
11	12	13	14	15	16	17	18	19	20
21	22	23	24	25	26	27	28	92	30
31	32	33	34	35	36	37	38	39	40
41	42	43	44	45	46	47	48	49	50
51	52	53	54	55	56	57	58	59	60
61	62	63	64	65	66	67	68	69	70
71	72	73	74	75	76	77	78	79	80
81	82	83	84	85	86	87	88	89	90
91	92	93	94	95	96	97	98	99	100

_____

_____

_____

_____

_____

_____

(77)

Name	**Date**

1. **a.** $3 + 4 =$ _____ **b.** $6 + 3 =$ _____ **c.** $5 + 0 =$ _____

    d. $10 - 2$ _____ **e.** $8 - 6 =$ _____ **f.** $4 - 3 =$ _____

    g. $20 - 15 =$ _____ **h.** $18 - 11 =$ _____ **i.** $13 - 9 =$ _____

    j. $4 + 15 =$ _____ **k.** $5 - 1 =$ _____ **l.** $7 + 31 =$ _____

    m. $22 + 48 =$ _____ **n.** $56 + 35 =$ _____ **o.** $82 + 16 =$ _____

    p. $99 - 42 =$ _____ **q.** $78 - 66 =$ _____ **r.** $63 - 27 =$ _____

2. Solve these problems using a calculator.

    a. Sue had 45 candies. Peter had 30 candies. How many more candies did Sue have?

    b. Maria has read 27 books. Adrian has read 32 books. How many books have they read altogether?

    ☐ $-$ ☐ $=$ ☐   ☐ $+$ ☐ $=$ ☐

3. Complete the number wheels.

    a. 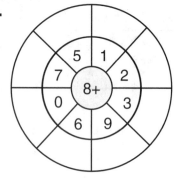   **b.** 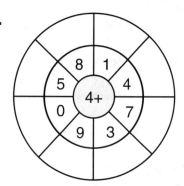   **c.**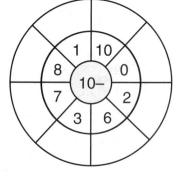

4. Use numbers  and signs ☐ $+$ ☐, ☐ $-$ ☐ to fill in the chart.

    You can use the numbers more than once.

    What is the biggest number you can get? _____

    What is the smallest number you can get? _____

working out

			=	
			=	
			=	
			=	
			=	
			=	

#8989 Targeting Math: Numeration and Fractions

Name   **Date**

All the numbers shown on your calculator are made from these shapes.

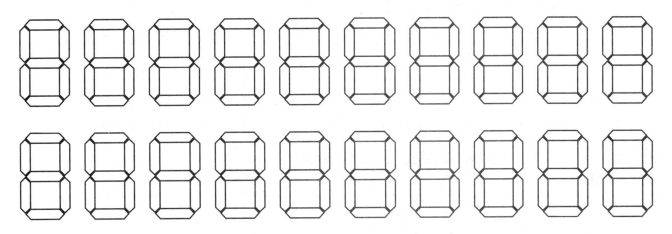

1. On the top row, color all the numbers from 0–9.

2. On the second row, try to color in your name.

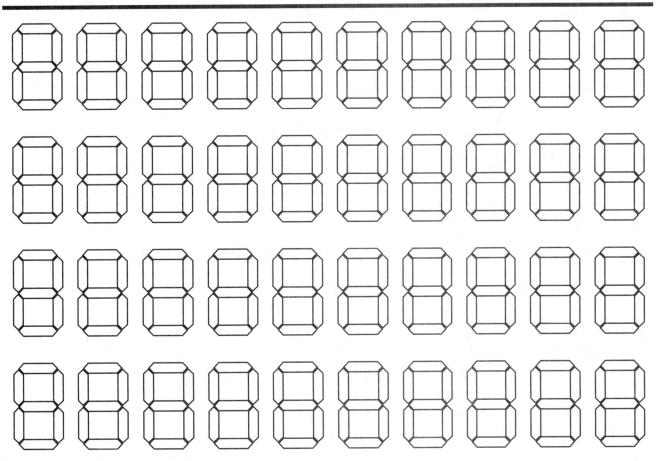

3. Make a pattern with numbers on these four rows. Use bright colors to make your pattern interesting.

(79)

Name	**Date**

You can make your calculator spell! If you turn your calculator upside down, some of the numbers look like letters.

Number	0	1	2	3	4	5	6	7	8	9
Letter	0	I	Z	E	h	S	g	L	B	G

Put each number into your calculator. Turn the calculator upside-down and look at the letters.

1. Which words do these numbers make?

   a. 805 _____   **b.** 604 _____

   c. 937 _____   **d.** 618 _____

   e. 345 _____   **f.** 733 _____

   g. 7735 _____   **h.** 3504 _____

   i. 5002 _____   **j.** 3080 _____

   k. 37818 _____   **l.** 372215 _____

   m. 577345 _____   **n.** 378806 _____

2. Now you can make up ten for a friend to do!

Number	Word		Number	Word
a. _____	_____	**b.** _____	_____
c. _____	_____	**d.** _____	_____
e. _____	_____	**f.** _____	_____
g. _____	_____	**h.** _____	_____
i. _____	_____	**j.** _____	_____

Name	**Date**

1. Making 9

The only keys working on your calculator are $\boxed{2}\ \boxed{+}\ \boxed{-}\ \boxed{x}\ \boxed{\div}\ \boxed{=}$

Using these keys, make 9. Write what you did.

_____

_____

2. Making 123

Without using the numbers 1, 2, 3, 4, 5, or 6, make the number 123 appear on your calculator. Write how you did it.

_____

_____

3. Making 10

You can only use the 8 key and operation keys to make your calculator show 10. Write how you did it.

_____

_____

4. Making the numbers 1–15.

This time the only keys working are $\boxed{2}\ \boxed{3}\ \boxed{x}\ \boxed{-}\ \boxed{+}\ \boxed{=}$.

Make all the numbers from 1–15 in as few operations as possible. Write how you made each number. (Example: $3 - 2 = 1$)

_____	_____
_____	_____
_____	_____
_____	_____
_____	_____
_____	_____
_____	

⑧⑴

ESTIMATION

Unit 2

**Estimating
Counting
Measuring
Perimeter
Comparing length
Money
Calculators**

Objectives

- estimates the areas of shapes using informal units
- recognizes and compares the sizes of groups through a variety of strategies such as estimating, matching one-to-one, and counting
- approximates, counts, compares, orders, and represents whole numbers and groups of objects to 100
- estimates the size of large collections by grouping the items
- uses number skills involving whole numbers to solve problems
- checks, using an alternative method if necessary, whether answers to problems are correct and sensible
- estimates, compares, orders, and measures the length of objects and the distances between objects using informal units
- uses available technology to explore basic mathematical concepts
- estimates the order of things by length and makes numerical estimates of length using a unit that can be seen or handled
- improves in judgments of order of length, area, mass, and capacity as a result of checking

Language

how many fit?, estimate, count, actual, how many altogether?, groups of 10, ones, number, answers, problems, check, calculator, unifix cubes, height, length, spent, exact amount

Materials/Resources

colored pencils, scissors, paste, Base 10 materials, calculators, unifix cubes, centimeter rulers

Contents of Student Pages

* Materials needed for each reproducible student page

Page 84 Estimating Area
measuring how many caterpillars fit on a leaf

* colored pencils, scissors, paste

Page 85 How Many?
estimate and count groups of objects

Page 86 Estimating Groups
estimating number of items in a picture and counting to check

* colored pencils

Page 87 Problem Solving
estimating answers to problems and checking by working them out; checking sums with a calculator; measuring perimeter with a centimeter ruler

* calculators, centimeter rulers

Page 88 Estimating Length
estimating heights and lengths and checking with a centimeter ruler

* centimeter rulers

Page 89 Estimating Money
estimating money spent and checking answers

* calculators

Page 90 Assessment
* centimeter rulers

Remember

- ❑ Students should be encouraged to estimate in all math strands and then check their estimates.
- ❑ Regularly check that students are showing some improvement in their estimation judgments.

Additional Activities

❏ As estimation is vital to informal and formal stages of measurement, provide many opportunities for students to estimate and then check in measuring activities.

❏ In other key learning areas, if math is integrated, provide estimating activities. (e.g., If painting a picture during art, have students estimate the length of their papers.)

❏ Try and have relevant estimation problems for the students. (e.g., "If everyone needs a book, how many do we need?")

❏ Have students design wrapping paper. Give them some boxes and encourage them to estimate the amount of paper needed to wrap the boxes.

❏ Encourage students to think of different ways to check their estimations.

❏ Provide students with catalogs. Items can be rounded off to the nearest dollar. Give students an amount to spend (e.g., $100). They have to cut out and paste the items onto a sheet of paper. They can then check to see how close to $100 they are.

❏ Pose problems (e.g., 340 + 620) and allow students to estimate, add, then check their answers with the aid of calculators.

❏ Play time games. Provide opportunities for students to estimate 1 minute, 5 minutes, 1 hour, etc. Ask questions, such as "How many times do you think you can clap your hands in 1 min.?"

❏ Play number estimation games (e.g., How many candies are in a packet? How many slices of bread in a loaf? How many biscuits in a packet?)

❏ Record estimates and actual numbers on charts. Allow the students to work in small groups. Let them choose a topic, estimate, and then find out the results. (e.g., How many cups of water are needed to fill a fish tank?) Groups can report their findings to the rest of the class.

Answers

Page 84 Estimating Area
1. Make sure it is a reasonable estimate.
2. Make sure leaf and caterpillars are colored.
3. Actual: 13 caterpillars

Page 85 How Many?
1. Make sure all estimates are reasonable. Actual answers are listed below.

a. 8   e. 6
b. 6   f. 8
c. 9   g. 10
d. 10   h. 7

2. Make sure estimate is reasonable. Actual: 64

Page 86 Estimating Groups
1. Make sure all estimates are reasonable.
2. a. 4   c. 16
    b. 9   d. 27
3. 7, 5, 75

Page 87 Problem Solving
Make sure all estimates are reasonable. Actual answers are listed below.

1. a. 84
   b. 29
   c. 90
   d. 44
2. a. 43
   b. 30
   c. 102
   d. 10
   e. 8
   f. 50
3. a. 16
   b. 20

Page 88 Estimating Length
Make sure all estimates are reasonable.

1. a. 8 centimeters
   b. 6 centimeters
   c. 5 centimeters
   d. 4 centimeters
2. a. 9   e. 6
   b. 4   f. 7
   c. 5   g. 11
   d. 10   h. 2

Page 89 Estimating Money
1. Make sure all estimates are reasonable. Actual answers are as follows: Nicky $5, Daniel $5, Grant $4, Susan $3
2. Make sure students check their answers with calculators.
3. Make sure the estimate is reasonable. Actual: $17

Page 90 Assessment
1. Make sure all estimates are reasonable. Actual answers are listed below.
   a. 7 cm   c. 4 cm
   b. 8 cm   d. 10 cm
2. Make sure all estimates are reasonable. Actual answers are listed below.
   a. $14   c. 9 cm
   b. 13   d. 66 flowers
3. Make sure all estimates are reasonable. Actual answers are listed below.
   a. 16 cm
   b. 70 cm
4. Make sure all estimates are reasonable. Actual answers are listed below.
   a. 54   d. 96
   b. 61   e. 14
   c. 19   f. 17

Name	**Date**

1. How many caterpillars do you think could fit on the leaf?

   Estimate _____

2. Color the caterpillars and the leaf.

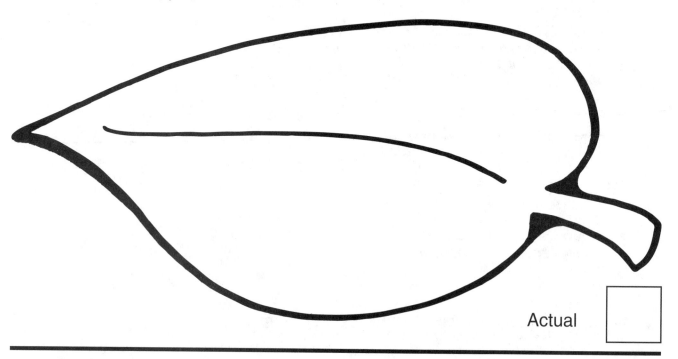

Actual

3. Cut out the caterpillars and see how many will fit onto the leaf. Write the actual answer in the box.

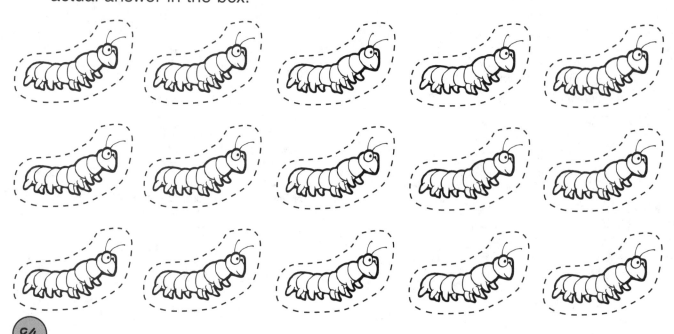

#8989 Targeting Math: Numeration and Fractions

Name	**Date**

1. Estimate and then count the items in each group.

		Estimate	**Actual**
a.			
b.			
c.			
d.			
e.			
f.			
g.			
h.			

2. Can you estimate how many items there are on this page altogether?

Estimate ☐   Actual ☐

85

Name	**Date**

1. From the drawing:

   a. estimate the number of rabbits.   _____

   b. estimate the number of mushrooms.   _____

   c. estimate the number of trees.   _____

   d. estimate the number of sheep.   _____

   e. estimate the number of birds.   _____

2. Count the:

   a. rabbits.   _____   **b.** mushrooms.   _____

   c. trees.   _____   **d.** sheep.   _____

3. Circle the birds in groups of 10, and count the groups of 10.

   _____

   Now, count the ones left over. _____

   How many birds altogether? _____

86

Name	**Date**

1. Estimate before working out the answers to these problems.

a. At the pool there were 46 boys and 38 girls. How many children were at the pool?

Estimate ☐   Actual ☐

b. There were 56 cows and horses in the field. If 27 were horses, how many cows were there?

Estimate ☐   Actual ☐

c. Next month 67 children will be 8 years old and 23 children will be 7 years old. How many children will have birthdays next month altogether?

Estimate ☐   Actual ☐

d. At recess 28 donuts and 16 muffins were bought. How many donuts and muffins were bought altogether?

Estimate ☐   Actual ☐

2. Estimate the answers to these questions and then check with a calculator.

	Estimate	Actual		Estimate	Actual
a. $67 - 24 =$	☐	☐	**b.** $6 + 24 =$	☐	☐
c. $89 + 13 =$	☐	☐	**d.** $19 - 9 =$	☐	☐
e. $12 - 4 =$	☐	☐	**f.** $36 + 14 =$	☐	☐

3. Estimate perimeters (the outer boundary) of these rectangles and then measure using a centimeter ruler.

a.

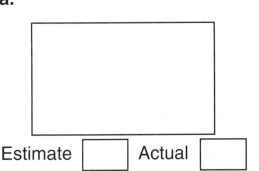

Estimate ☐   Actual ☐

b.

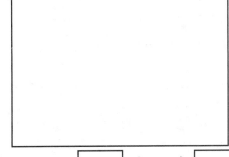

Estimate ☐   Actual ☐

Name	**Date**

1. Estimate the heights using centimeters and then check.

a.	**b.**	**c.**	**d.**

Estimate _____	Estimate _____	Estimate _____	Estimate _____
Actual _____	Actual _____	Actual _____	Actual _____

2. Join each problem to an estimate located in the box. Then measure using centimeters.

a. ‒◯‒◯‒◯‒◯‒◯‒◯‒◯‒◯‒◯‒◯‒◯‒◯‒◯‒◯‒ 　　　　**b.** ‒◯‒◯‒◯‒◯‒◯‒◯‒

　　　　　　　Actual: _____ 　　　　　　　　　　　　　　　Actual: _____

c. ◯‒◯‒◯‒◯‒◯‒◯‒◯‒◯‒◯ 　**d.** ◯‒◯‒◯‒◯‒◯‒◯‒◯‒◯‒◯‒◯‒◯‒◯‒◯‒◯‒◯‒

　　　　Actual: _____ 　　　　　　　　　　　　　　　　　Actual: _____

Estimates	6	2	5	9	10	11	7	4

e. ◯‒◯‒◯‒◯‒◯‒◯‒◯‒◯‒◯‒◯‒ 　　　　**f.** ◯‒◯‒◯‒◯‒◯‒◯‒◯‒◯‒◯‒◯‒◯‒◯‒

　　　　Actual: _____ 　　　　　　　　　　　　　　　　Actual: _____

g. ◯‒◯‒◯‒◯‒◯‒◯‒◯‒◯‒◯‒◯‒◯‒◯‒◯‒◯‒◯‒◯‒ 　　　　**h.** ◯‒◯‒◯‒

88　　Actual: _____ 　　　　　　　　　　　　　　　Actual: _____

Name	**Date**

1. Four friends went to the football game. Estimate how much they each spent.

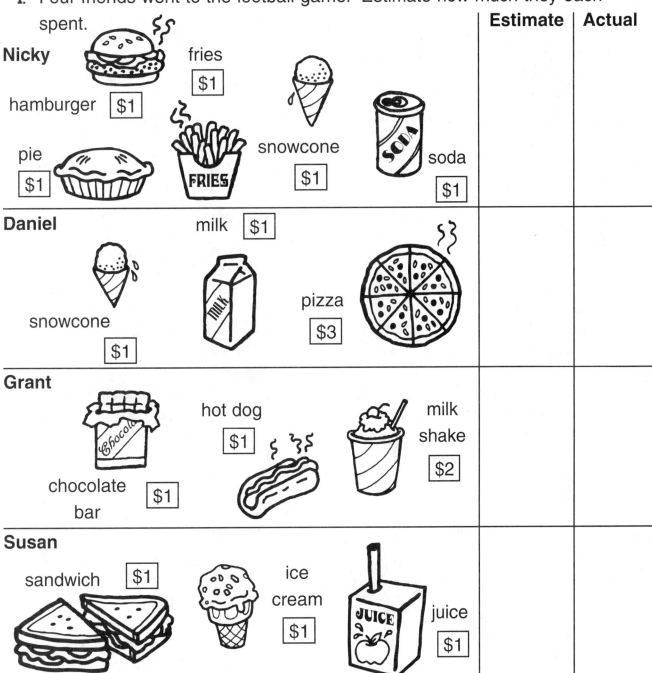

	Estimate	**Actual**
Nicky		
hamburger $1, fries $1, pie $1, snowcone $1, soda $1		
Daniel		
snowcone $1, milk $1, pizza $3		
Grant		
chocolate bar $1, hot dog $1, milk shake $2		
Susan		
sandwich $1, ice cream $1, juice $1		

2. Use a calculator to check each one.

3. How much did they spend altogether?

Estimate _____   Actual _____

89

Name	**Date**

1. Estimate the lengths of the leaves in centimeters and then check using a centimeter ruler.

   a.

   Estimate [   ] Actual [   ]   Estimate [   ] Actual [   ]

   b.

   c.    **d.**

   Estimate [   ] Actual [   ]   Estimate [   ] Actual [   ]

2. Estimate the answers to these problems and then find the actual answers.

   a. Kate had $5. If she was given $9, how much money does she have?
   Estimate _____
   Actual _____

   b. If George had 30 marbles and lost 17 marbles, how many does he now have?
   Estimate _____
   Actual _____

   c. A piece of string is 20 cm long and Ty cuts off 11 cm. How many centimeters of string does Ty have left over?
   Estimate _____
   Actual _____

   d. In Lamia's garden there are 43 daffodils and 23 pansies. How many flowers are there in Lamia's garden?
   Estimate _____
   Actual _____

3. Estimate the perimeters of the boxes and then find the perimeters using a calculator.

   a.
   3 cm
   5 cm
   Estimate [   ]
   Actual [   ]

   b.
   25 cm
   10 cm
   Estimate [   ]
   Actual [   ]

4. Estimate the answers and then check using a calculator.

   a. 96 − 42 =
   Estimate _____
   Actual _____

   b. 27 + 34 =
   Estimate _____
   Actual _____

   c. 5 + 14 =
   Estimate _____
   Actual _____

   d. 71 + 25 =
   Estimate _____
   Actual _____

   e. 29 − 15 =
   Estimate _____
   Actual _____

   f. 89 − 72 =
   Estimate _____
   Actual _____

FRACTIONS

Grouping, finding halves and quarters, estimating halves and quarters, drawing and naming parts of groups, and matching parts of groups to labels are all skills practiced in these units.

Correct language is encouraged is encouraged when describing, reading, naming, and writing fractions. Students relate fractions to everyday situations. They draw to solve fraction problems and both draw and interpret graphs to represent parts of a group. The activity page is making designs based on halves. Two assessment pages have been included.

BEGINNING FRACTIONS

Unit 1

Parts of a group
Remainders
Half
Graphs

Objectives

- describes and models the relationships between the parts and the whole
- recognizes and compares the sizes of groups through a variety of strategies such as estimating, matching, one-to-one, counting
- uses number skills involving whole numbers to solve problems
- uses informal fraction language in relation to objects and collections of objects

Language

out of, groups, match, record, parts, are not shaded, less than one half, how many, correct group, graph

Materials/Resources

colored pencils, (optional: paint, scissors, paste)

Contents of Student Pages

* *Materials needed for each reproducible student page*

Remember

❑ *Give students many opportunities to develop the concept of parts of a group, before being formally introduced to "one half."*

Additional Activities

❑ *Incidentally use fraction "language" wherever possible such as whole, half. (e.g., "Let's cut the apple into halves.")*

❑ *Have students paint blobs. Students fold the paper into half, unfold paper, paint on one half, fold it over, unfold, and get a symmetrical design.*

❑ *Provide students with catalogs and magazines. Encourage them to find "halves." These can be pasted onto wall charts or put into class books.*

❑ *Choose a number such as 4. Students find groups of 4 in catalogs and magazines. Parts can be circled and labeled. (e.g., 2 out of 4 or 1 out of 4) They can be pasted into class books or on wall charts.*

❑ *Provide sorting materials and encourage students to describe their collections as parts of a group. (e.g., "There are 4 cars. One out of the 4 is black and 3 out of the 4 are red.")*

❑ *In creative arts, provide opportunities for printing with halves. (e.g., apples, potatoes)*

❑ *Provide opportunities for the students to develop an understanding of sharing and "fair share."*

❑ *Take advantage of everyday situations to emphasize fraction concepts. (e.g., "There are four away today. Three out of the four are girls.")*

❑ *Make "fraction" pies out of different-colored paper stuck onto cardboard.*

Answers

Page 94 Parts of a Group

1. Make sure 8 out of 10 fish are colored red.
2. Make sure 4 out of 8 sea snails are colored yellow.
3. Make sure 5 out of 6 sea slugs are colored orange.
4. Make sure 3 out of 4 clams are colored red.
5. Make sure all octopi (2) are colored pink.
6. Make sure 6 out of 9 starfish are colored blue.
7. Make sure 7 out of 7 kelp are colored green.
8. Make sure 4 out of 5 rocks are colored brown.
9. Make sure 2 out of 3 sharks are colored orange.

Page 95 Naming Parts

1. a. Make sure 6 balloons are colored and 4 are not colored. 4, 10
   b. Make sure 4 caterpillars are colored and 6 are not colored. 6, 10
   c. Make sure 14 beads are colored and 6 are not colored. 6, 20
   d. Mare sure 11 flowers are colored and 9 are not colored. 9, 20
2. a. Make sure 7 donuts are circled.
   b. Make sure 9 pencils are circled.
3. a. Teacher to check.
   b. Teacher to check.

Page 96 Estimating

1. a. about one half
   b. more than one half
   c. less than one half
   d. about one half
   e. less than one half
   f. about one half
   g. more than one half
   h. less than one half
2. a. Make sure one half of the pizza is colored.
   b. Make sure one half of the square is colored.

Page 97 Parts of Groups

1. a. 7 tissue boxes should be colored.
   b. 3 bags of dog food should be colored.
   c. 5 cans of peaches should be colored.
   d. 15 cans of tuna should be colored.
   e. 6 cans of soda should be colored.
   f. 4 boxes of cereal should be colored.
   g. 12 cans of beans should be colored.
   h. 4 cans of corn should be colored.
   i. 10 boxes of Sudsy Soap should be colored.
   j. 5 cans of chips should be colored.
2. a. 1   e. 6   i. 3
   b. 1   f. 5   j. 1
   c. 5   g. 1
   d. 3   h. 5

Page 98 Matching

1. 6 out of 8   5. 6 out of 10   9. 3 out of 8
2. 4 out of 6   6. 6 out of 9   10. 3 out of 6
3. 4 out of 9   7. 5 out of 6
4. 4 out of 8   8. 8 out of 10

Page 99 Graphs

1. a. 9 out of 28   d. 19 out of 28
   b. 11 out of 28   e. 17 out of 28
   c. 8 out of 28   f. 20 out of 28
2. Teacher to check

Page 100 Assessment

1. a. 2 out of 6   c. 4 out of 7
   b. 1 out of 3   d. 3 out of 5
2. a. Three squares should be colored.
   b. One half of the shape should be colored.
   c. Two parts of the shape should be colored.
   d. All parts of the shape should be colored.
   e. Three parts of the shape should be colored.
   f. One part of the shape should be colored.
   g. Five parts of the shape should be colored.
   h. Eight parts of the shape should be colored.
3. a. 1 out of 4   c. 6 out of 12
   b. 2 out of 3   d. 2 out of 4
4. Make sure half of all shapes are colored.
5. a. 1 leaf should be colored.
   b. 3 drops should be colored.
   c. 8 acorns should be colored.
   d. 6 flowers should be colored.

Page 101 Design Time Activity

Make sure half of all shapes are colored.
Make sure each design is different.

Name	Date

1. Color 8 out of 10 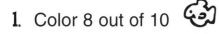 red.

2. Color 4 out of 8 yellow.

3. Color 5 out of 6 orange.

4. Color 3 out of 4 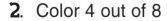 red.

5. Color 2 out of 2 pink.

6. Color 6 out of 9 blue.

7. Color 7 out of 7 green.

8. Color 4 out of 5 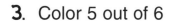 brown.

9. Color 2 out of 3 orange.

#8989 Targeting Math: Numeration and Fractions

Name	**Date**

1. Color the parts to match the labels. Record the uncolored parts.

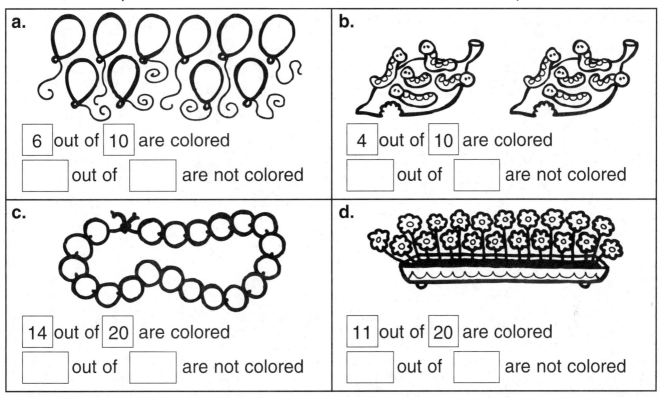

a.

6 out of 10 are colored

☐ out of ☐ are not colored

b.

4 out of 10 are colored

☐ out of ☐ are not colored

c.

14 out of 20 are colored

☐ out of ☐ are not colored

d.

11 out of 20 are colored

☐ out of ☐ are not colored

2. Circle the groups and then color.

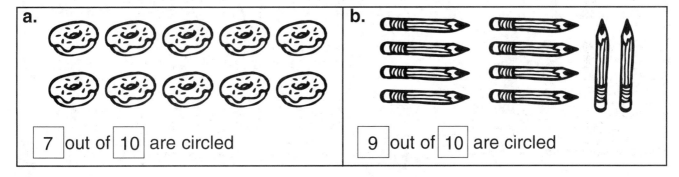

a.

7 out of 10 are circled

b.

9 out of 10 are circled

3. Draw your own groups. Circle some parts.

a.

☐ out of ☐ are not circled

b.

☐ out of ☐ are not circled

95

| Name | Date |

1. Color the correct answer.

a.

| less than one half |
| about one half |
| more than one half |

b.

| less than one half |
| about one half |
| more than one half |

c.

| less than one half |
| about one half |
| more than one half |

d.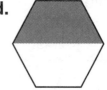

| less than one half |
| about one half |
| more than one half |

e.

| less than one half |
| about one half |
| more than one half |

f.

| less than one half |
| about one half |
| more than one half |

g.

| less than one half |
| about one half |
| more than one half |

h.

| less than one half |
| about one half |
| more than one half |

2. **a.** Color one half of the pizza.

b. Color one half of the square.

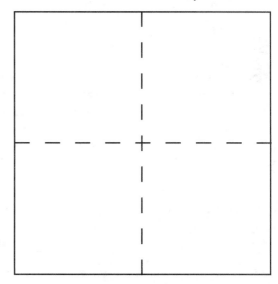

96

Name   **Date**

1. Color.

   a. 7 out of 8 tissue boxes   **b.** 3 out of 4 bags of dog food

   c. 5 out of 8 cans of peaches   **d.** 15 out of 20 cans of tuna

   e. 6 out of 12 cans of soda   **f.** 4 out of 5 boxes of cereal

   g. 12 out of 17 cans of beans   **h.** 4 out of 7 cans of corn

   i. 10 out of 15 boxes of Sudsy Soap **j.** 5 out of 6 cans of chips

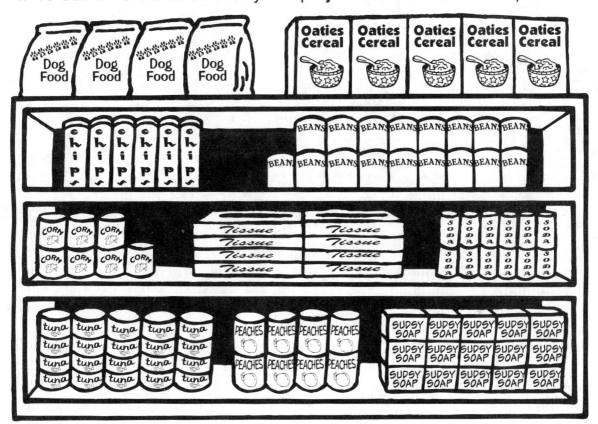

2. How many are not colored?

   a. boxes of cereal   _____   **f.** cans of beans   _____

   b. chip cans   _____   **g.** boxes of tissues   _____

   c. boxes of Sudsy Soap _____   **h.** cans of tuna   _____

   d. cans of peaches   _____   **i.** cans of corn   _____

   e. cans of soda   _____   **j.** bags of dog food   _____

                        #8989 Targeting Math: Numeration and Fractions

Name	Date

Use a different color to match each picture to the correct number sentence.

1.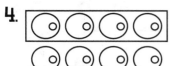

buttons

2.

balls

3.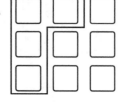

squares

4.

beads

5.

coins

6.

candies

7.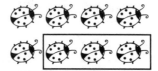

ice-cream cones

8.

balloons

9.

ladybugs

10.

snails

4 out of 6

6 out of 8

4 out of 8

4 out of 9

8 out of 10

5 out of 6

3 out of 6

6 out of 10

3 out of 8

6 out of 9

#8989 Targeting Math: Numeration and Fractions

Name	**Date**

1. Complete the sentences.

   Student Eye Colors

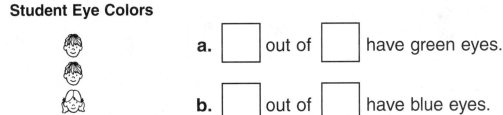

green   **blue**   **brown**

a. ☐ out of ☐ have green eyes.

b. ☐ out of ☐ have blue eyes.

c. ☐ out of ☐ have brown eyes.

d. ☐ out of ☐ don't have green eyes.

e. ☐ out of ☐ don't have blue eyes.

f. ☐ out of ☐ don't have brown eyes.

2. Survey your class and make a graph of hair colors. Complete the sentences.

   Hair Colors

a. ☐ out of ☐ have blonde hair.

b. ☐ out of ☐ have brown hair.

c. ☐ out of ☐ have black hair.

d. ☐ out of ☐ don't have red hair.

e. ☐ out of ☐ don't have blonde hair.

f. ☐ out of ☐ don't have red hair.

g. ☐ out of ☐ don't have black hair.

blonde   brown   black   red

99

Name	**Date**

1. What part of each group is circled?

a.    b.    c.    d.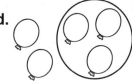

___ out of ___   ___ out of ___   ___ out of ___   ___ out of ___

2. Color the part of the shape to match the label.

a.    b. 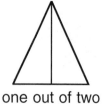   c. 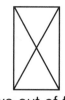   d.

three out of eight   one out of two   two out of four   four out of four

e. 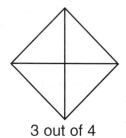   f.    g.   h.

3 out of 4   1 out of 3   5 out of six   8 out of 12

3. What part is shaded?

a. 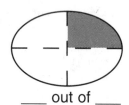   b. 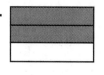   c. 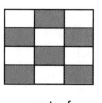   d.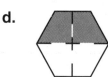

___ out of ___   ___ out of ___   ___ out of ___   ___ out of ___

4. Color half of each shape.

a. 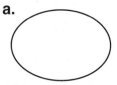   b. 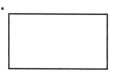   c.   d.   e.   f.

5. Color.

a.   b.   c.   d.

1 out of 2   3 out of 4   8 out of 10   6 out of 8

Name	**Date**

Each of these square cakes has been cut into 8 pieces. Make designs by coloring the icing. Color exactly half of each cake. Make the design different each time.

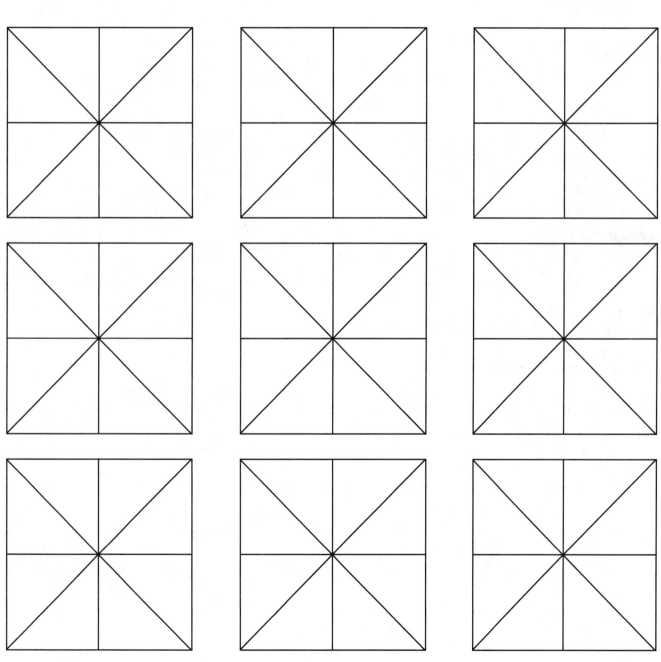

MORE FRACTIONS

Unit 2

Halves
Counting
Quarters, thirds
Drawing problems
Writing problems
Solving problems

Objectives

- *describes and models the relationships between the parts and the whole*
- *uses number skills involving whole numbers to solve problems*
- *recognizes and compares the sizes of groups through a variety of strategies such as estimating, matching, one-to-one, and counting*
- *engages in writing texts with the intention of conveying an idea or message*

Language

count, how many?, 1/2, 1/4, 1/3, quarters, divide, third, quarter, halves, thirds, correct, problem, solve, one quarter, one half

Materials/Resources

colored pencils, (optional: geoboards, rubber bands)

Contents of Student Pages

* *Materials needed for each reproducible student page*

Page 104 Halves
identifying half of groups 2–20; counting how many in each group

* *colored pencils*

Page 105 Matching Fractions
matching group with fraction label

Page 106 Quarters
identifying quarters of groups 4–20; drawing groups and dividing into quarters

* *colored pencils*

Page 107 Correct Labels
identifying groups and parts that are/are not 1/2 or 1/4; matching circle fractions with fraction labels; drawing parts on fractions

Page 108 Halves and Quarters
drawing to solve fraction problems

* *colored pencils*

Page 109 Problem Solving
coloring objects to solve fraction problems; writing a fraction problem

* *colored pencils*

Page 110 Assessment

Remember

❑ *Don't introduce a new fraction until students have a good understanding of ones already taught.*

Additional Activities

❑ Have a "fraction" feast. Make sandwiches with the students and cut into halves and quarters. Cut bread into quarters or small pizzas into quarters.

❑ Encourage students to make shapes with geoboards and then divide them into halves or quarters using rubber bands. Students can record their findings.

❑ Give students 1 cm-squared paper and encourage them to draw shapes and then divide them into fractions.

❑ Use graphs to develop fraction concepts. (e.g., "Nine out of 28 get driven to school, 10 out of 28 get the bus, 9 out of 28 walk to school")

❑ Provide students with colored paper. Get them to draw shapes and then divide them into halves. These can be cut out, pasted onto paper, and displayed.

❑ Pose problems with concrete materials. (e.g., Put 6 apples out, then put 3 in a bowl. Ask, "Have half been put in the bowl?")

❑ Make simple fraction story problems and use as models to encourage students to make some to share with the rest of the class.

❑ Pose problems. For example, "How many ways can you divide shapes into half (quarters, etc.)?" Give them paper to find out by drawing. Use circles, squares, rectangles and other shapes.

Answers

Page 104 Halves
1. Make sure items are colored according to answers in Number 2.
2. clouds 3, sheep 10, bees 2, balloons 6, chickens 9, children 1, flowers 7, birds 4, trees 8, snails 5

Page 105 Matching Fractions

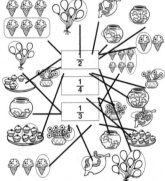

Page 106 Quarters
1. a. Each flower should be circled. One flower should be colored.
   b. Two boats in each circle. Two boats should be colored.
   c. Each leaf should be circled. One leaf should be colored.
   d. Three gems in each circle. Three gems should be colored.
   e. One umbrella in each circle. One umbrella should be colored.
   f. Three apples in each circle. Three apples should be colored.

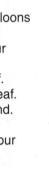

g. Five balls in each circle. Five balls should be colored.
   h. Two coins in each circle. Two coins should be colored.
   i. Four squares in each circle. Four squares should be colored.
2. a.–c. Make sure objects have been circled into quarters.

Page 107 Correct Labels
1. a. Checkmark
   b. No checkmark
   c. No checkmark
   d. Checkmark
2. a. Checkmark
   b. Checkmark
   c. No checkmark
   d. No checkmark
3. Shapes left to right: quarters, whole, halves, thirds
4. a. Six balloons should have strings.
   b. Three balloons should have strings.
   c. Four balloons should have strings.

Page 108 Halves and Quarters
1. Two balloons should have strings. Two balloons should not have strings.
2. Four cakes should be on a blue plate. Four cakes should be on a yellow plate.
3. Three snails should be drawn on a big leaf. Three snails should be drawn on a small leaf. Three snails should be drawn on the ground. Three are not drawn yet.
4. Four apples should be drawn on a tree. Four apples should be on the ground.
5. Three sheep should be in each paddock.

Page 109 Problem Solving
1. a. 4
   b. white 8, red 4, blue 4
   c. red 2, blue 2, yellow 2
2. Teacher to check.
3. a. red 4, blue 2, yellow 2
   b. red 4, blue 0, yellow 4
   c. red 2, blue 4, yellow 2

Page 110 Assessment
1. a. One sheep should be circled.
   b. Four boats should be circled.
   c. Two baseballs should be circled.
2. a. Two snails should be circled.
   b. Four light bulbs should be circled.
3. a. Three boats should have flags.
   b. Two hives should each have a bee.
   c. Two balloons should each have strings.
   d. One hat should be on a child.
4. a. Make sure the oval has four equal parts and one part shaded in.
   b. Make sure the rectangle has two equal parts and one part shaded in.
   c. Make sure circle has four equal parts and one part shaded in.
   d. Make sure shape has two equal parts and one part shaded in.
   e. Make sure shape has four equal parts and one part shaded in.
5. a. red 6, blue 3, yellow 3
   b. Four snails should be drawn on the leaf. Four snails should be drawn not on the leaf.

Name	Date

1. Count and then color half the number of each object.

2. How many did you color?

clouds ☐   sheep ☐   bees ☐

balloons ☐   chickens ☐   children ☐

flowers ☐   birds ☐   trees ☐

snails ☐

Name	Date

Match to the correct fraction.

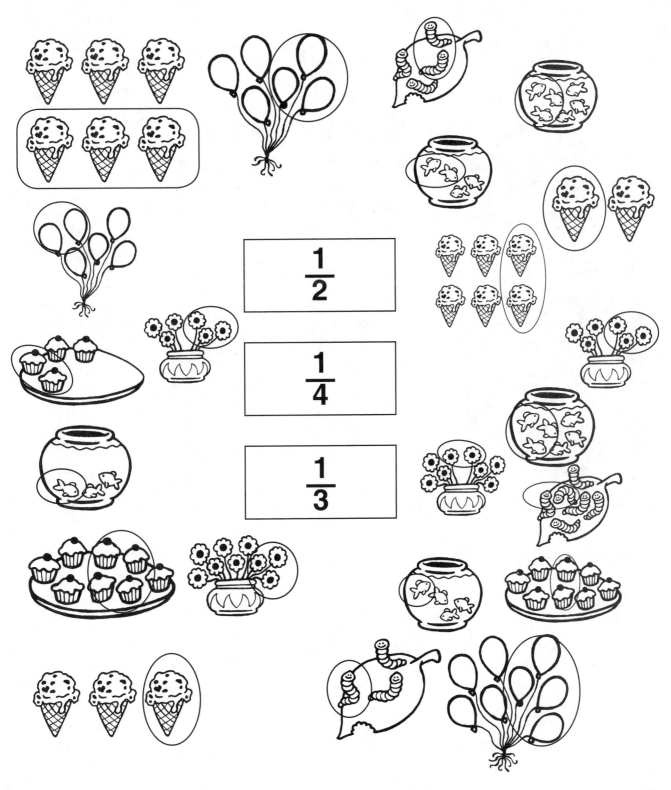

Name	**Date**

1. Circle to make into quarters, then color one quarter.

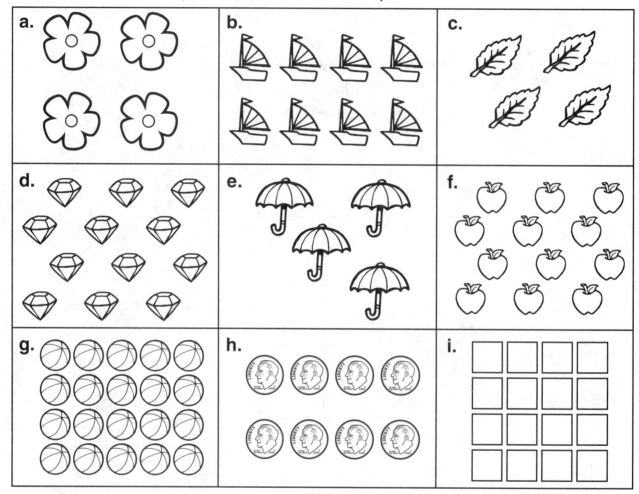

2. Draw objects and then group into quarters.

   a.   b.   c.

Name　　　　　　　　　　　　　　　　　　　**Date**

1. Place a checkmark by the fraction if the correct area is shaded.

   a. 　　　**b.** 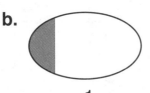　　　**c.** 　　　**d.**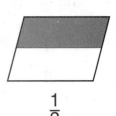

   $\frac{1}{2}$　　　　　　$\frac{1}{2}$　　　　　　$\frac{1}{2}$　　　　　　$\frac{1}{2}$

2. Place a checkmark if the correct group is circled.

   a. 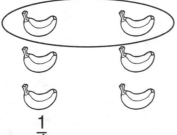　　　　　**b.**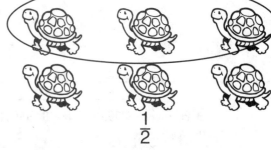

   $\frac{1}{4}$　　　　　　　　　　　$\frac{1}{2}$

   c. 　　　　　**d.**

   $\frac{1}{4}$　　　　　　　　　　　$\frac{1}{4}$

3. Match the picture with the label.

   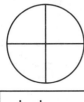　　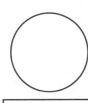　　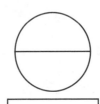　　

   | halves | whole | quarters | thirds |

4. **a.** Draw strings on half the balloons.

   b. Draw strings on a quarter of the balloons.

   c. Draw strings on a third of the balloons.

107

Name	**Date**

Draw pictures to solve these problems.

1. There are 4 balloons. Half are on strings, and the other half are not on strings.

2. There are 8 cakes. Half are on a blue plate, and the other half are on a yellow plate.

3. There are 12 snails. A quarter are on a big leaf. A quarter are on a small leaf and a quarter are on the ground.

   How many are not drawn yet? _____

   Draw the leaves and the snails on them.

4. There are 8 apples. Draw half on a tree and the other half on the ground.

5. There are 6 sheep. Draw half in one paddock and the other half in another paddock.

#8989 Targeting Math: Numeration and Fractions

Name	**Date**

1. Color to solve the problems.

a.

Half the sheep are white and the rest are black.

How many sheep are black? _____

b.

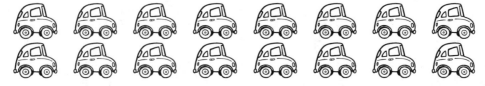

Half the cars in the car park are white, one quarter are red, and one quarter are blue.

How many cars are white? _____   How many cars are red? _____

How many cars are blue?_____

c. A third of the flowers are red, a third of the flowers are blue, and a third are yellow. How many flowers are red _____, blue _____, yellow _____?

2. Write your own problem.

_____

_____

_____

3. Read the directions in the box below. Color the shapes and solve the problem.

HOW MANY?

a. red _____ blue _____ yellow _____

b. red _____ blue _____ yellow _____

c. red _____ blue _____ yellow _____

One half of the circles and squares are red.
One quarter of the circles are blue, and one half of the triangles are blue.
One quarter of the circles are yellow and one half of the squares are yellow.
One quarter of the triangles are red.
One quarter of the triangles are yellow.

(109)

Name	**Date**

1. Circle a half of each group.

   a.
   b.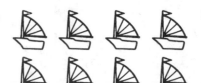
   c.

2. Circle a quarter of each group.

   a.
   b.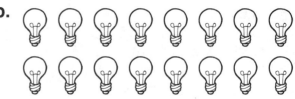

3. **a.** Put flags on half the boats.

   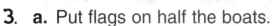

   b. Draw a bee on half the hives.

   c. Draw strings on a quarter of the balloons.

   d. Put hats on a quarter of the children.

4. Draw lines and shade to show:

   a. $\frac{1}{4}$

   b.  $\frac{1}{2}$

   c. $\frac{1}{4}$

   d. $\frac{1}{2}$

   e. $\frac{1}{4}$

5. Solve the problems.

   a.

   Color half the fish red.
   Color a quarter of the fish yellow.
   Color a quarter of the fish blue.
   How many fish are red? _____
   How many fish are blue? _____
   How many fish are yellow? _____

   b. There are 8 snails. Draw half of them on the leaf and the other half not on the leaf.

Skills Index

The following index lists specific objectives for the student pages of each unit in the book. The objectives are grouped according to the sections listed in the Table of Contents. Use the Skills Index as a resource for identifying the units and student pages you wish to use.

Calculators

accurately presses a given sequence of buttons (Pages: 72, 73, 74)

approximates, counts, compares, orders, and represents whole numbers and groups of objects up to 100 (Page: 77)

recognizes what works and what did not work while answering mathematical questions (Page: 75)

represents numbers in a variety of forms, including the use of a calculator (Page: 73)

uses a calculator to represent and explore numbers, place value, and operations (Page: 76)

uses a calculator to record numbers and to explore counting sequences (Page: 77)

uses the available technology to explore mathematical concepts (Page: 72)

uses available technology to help in the solution of mathematical problems (Pages: 73, 74)

writes complete number sentences using one of the + − and = signs (Page: 75)

Estimation

approximates, counts, compares, orders, and represents whole numbers and groups of objects to 100 (Page: 86)

checks using an alternative method if necessary, whether answers to problems are correct and sensible (Page: 88)

estimates the areas of shapes using informal units (Page: 84)

estimates, compares, orders, and measures the length of objects and the distances between objects using informal units (Pages: 87, 88)

estimates the order of things by length and makes numerical estimates of length using a unit that can be seen or handled (Page: 88)

estimates the size of large collections by grouping the items (Page: 86)

improves in judgments of order of length and capacity as a result of checking (Page: 88)

recognizes and compares the sizes of groups through a variety of strategies such as estimating, matching one-to-one, and counting (Pages: 85, 86)

uses the available technology to explore basic mathematical concepts (Page: 87)

uses number skills involving whole numbers to solve problems (Pages: 87, 89)

Fractions

describes and models the relationships between the parts and the whole (Pages: 94, 95, 96, 97, 98, 99, 104, 105, 106, 107, 108, 109)

recognizes and compares the sizes of groups through a variety of strategies such as estimating, matching, one-to-one, counting (Pages: 94, 104, 105, 106)

uses informal fraction language in relation to objects and collections of objects (Pages: 95, 97, 98, 99)

uses number skills involving whole numbers to solve problems (Pages: 95, 97, 99, 104, 108, 109)

engages in writing texts with the intention of conveying an idea or message (Page: 109)

Numeration

answers mathematical questions using pictures and imagery (Pages: 30, 32)

comments on information in displays produced by himself or herself and others (Page: 64)

counts forward in 1s (Page: 12)

counts forwards and backwards by 1s from any number in range 0–20 (Page: 21)

counts in 2s (Page: 24)

counts forwards up to 20 (Pages: 30, 32)

counts forwards up to 100 (Page: 34)

counts backwards from 20 (Page: 23)

Skills Index

Numeration *(cont.)*

counts forwards and backwards starting from any whole number (Page: 31)

counts by ones, twos, fives, or tens both forwards and backwards (Pages: 40, 41, 42, 43, 44)

counts forwards and backwards up to 1,000 in 1s, 10s and 100s starting from any whole number (Pages: 51, 62)

counts, compares, and orders whole numbers up to 999 and represents them in symbols and words stating the place value of any digit (Pages: 52, 54, 61, 62, 63, 65, 66)

demonstrates an understanding that numbers can be represented using groupings of 10, 100, and 1,000 (Page: 53)

estimates and calculates mentally, including adding and subtracting 10 (Page: 41)

estimates the size of larger collections by grouping the items (Page: 51)

follows simple directions (Page: 10)

identifies, continues, and invents whole number patterns (Page: 45)

generates and represents repeating or simple counting number patterns (Page: 62)

makes groups of up to ten objects (Pages: 9, 10, 11, 22)

makes groups of a given size (Pages: 9, 10, 11, 22)

makes, names, records, and renames numbers up to 999 (Pages: 50, 51)

matches numerals to the appropriate group (Page: 8)

names and records numbers up to 100 (Pages: 33, 43)

obtains and tests rules to continue number sequences (Page: 40)

orders groups according to the number of objects (Pages: 13, 24)

orders and represents whole numbers up to 100 (Pages: 31, 33, 34, 43)

orders whole numbers by counting forwards and backwards up to 100 (Page: 41)

orders whole numbers up to 999 (Pages: 50, 64)

recognizes numerals 0 to 10 (Pages: 9, 10)

recognizes numerals from 0–20 (Page: 23)

recognizes numeral names zero to ten (Pages: 11, 22)

recognizes patterns in lines of a hundreds chart (Page: 42)

says numeral names in correct sequence (Pages: 10, 13)

says number names/numerals to 10 in correct sequence (Page: 21)

says number names/numerals to 20 in correct sequence (Pages: 23, 24)

selects and carries out the operation appropriate to situations involving addition or sorts and describes objects in terms of their features, such as size and shape (Page: 64)

subtraction (Pages: 45, 46, 74, 76, 87)

understands ordinals and their sequence (Page: 19)

uses appropriate mathematical language (Page: 19)

uses a calculator to explore basic mathematical concepts (Pages: 45, 63)

uses number skills involving whole numbers to solve problems (Pages: 35, 55)

uses and recognizes the ordinal names from 1st to 10th (Page: 20)

uses language of odd and even (Page: 24)

uses materials and models to develop part-whole understanding of numbers (Pages: 52, 53, 54, 65)